She has an amazing energy that is contagious and makes everyone around her smile. She brings so much joy and happiness to a classroom. That made me excited and ready to take on the rest of my day.

-Lynsey Naugle

What People Are Saying About
Dr. Chrissy Whiting-Madison

Dr. Chrissy is a fantastic writer and speaker! I've heard her speak several times and am actively using her methods toward being happier! It really does work. She has helped me make really simple changes that make me feel so much happier and more fulfilled. I love you Dr. Chrissy!

-Ra Butler, Monster Art Mission

No matter how seemingly difficult it's ever been to feel welcome in a large group, never have I been in the presence of Dr. Whiting-Madison speaking and didn't feel as though I was completely welcome and understood in every way, if not celebrated for my differences.

-Alya Al-Taweel

Dr. Chrissy has always been bubbly and bright with a contagious laugh!

-Chris Lee

Chrissy is one of those people who, even if you don't know her, you see her and you can't help but smile because of how happy she looks. I can tell you many times I would get off of work and go to class completely exhausted and feeling "checked out" for the day, but sure enough every time I got there and saw how happy and excited Chrissy was to teach us I couldn't help but be excited for what we were going to learn that night regardless of how tired I felt.

She has this rejuvenating energy about her that is 1000% contagious. Her energy not only got me pumped for class but I feel like I retained the information much better because of her happy energy surrounding her job and students. I took a couple classes while attending LU, and hers is the only one I remember vividly because of her energy and way of being. I can truly say I never had a bad night of class because of her contagious happy go lucky energy.

-Britnee Summers

Chrissy is one of those people that always brightens up the room with her eccentric and bubbly personality. She always has a smile on her face and puts sunshine into the life of others.

-Andrea Fetsch

Chrissy is one of the kindest, warmest and friendliness human beings I have ever met. She genuinely cares about everyone she comes into contact with. I've never had a more caring and loving college professor in my life!

-Amanda Jo Johnson

Chrissy is someone who can make you feel instantly comfortable. In her presence, you just know that you're safe to feel as happy or as sad as you want and she'll never let you feel alone. She can make someone feel significant, even if she doesn't know their name.

-Cheryl Trueblood

Her positivity is absolutely contagious.

-Amanda Hollenbeck

Even if you're having a bad day, Chrissy will always bring light into your day.

-Kasi VanSandt

Choosing Happiness

Dr. Chrissy Whiting-Madison

www.TotalPublishingAndMedia.com

ISBN 978-1-63302-118-1

Dedication

This book is dedicated to my biggest supporters:

My husband, Matthew, who embraces our crazy life and encourages me with more love and patience than you can possibly imagine.

My daughter, Carina Ann, who is the most amazing child with a heart of gold. I am so proud to be your mom! You are my greatest blessing!

Last, but not least, my mom, Shirley. My mom has been my rock and biggest cheerleader my entire life. Where would I be without you?

I also want to acknowledge my incredible friends and students who teach me more about happiness every single day. You all make my life so much better!

Table of Contents

Why Read This Book?

When people meet me, I often get very strange reactions. Sometimes they brighten up and return my smile and sometimes they look uncomfortable. Sometimes they are startled, yet despite this variation in reaction one thing remains consistent. People always want to know more.

I am frequently asked the same question,

"How do you do it? How do you stay so positive all the time?"

This book is all about how I do it. How I shake off the negative and embrace the positives. I am sharing my secrets with the world.

I often encounter skeptics. These people seem to think I am fake or insincere, but this book is set to let you know I am "for real." You can be "for real" too.

Everyone deserves to be happy, or at least happier. Happiness should never be elusive or restricted to those with immense wealth or professional success. This book tells you how to make easy, small changes in routines which will lead to huge changes in your life - satisfaction and overall joy.

This book will change your life, just like the practices changed mine. Get ready to be happy.

Acknowledgements

Many thanks go to Matt, for your patience and enduring love while I have prattled on and on about happiness and positive psychology. Thank you for loving and supporting me.

Also, much appreciation goes out to my beloved students, if it weren't for your endless support and encouragement of my unique brand of "eccentricity" I would never be where I am today.

Finally thank you to my dearest friends-Heather K, Bill K, Suzanne, John, Heather S, Ra, Alex, Michelle, Randy, Naomi, Genie, Miranda, and Amy. Thank you for loving me when I didn't love myself.

Foreword

As I have lived and experienced the first 40 years of my life, one thing has remained a constant. Many people are not happy. Another thing I have learned is misery does indeed love company. In other words, when people are not happy, they do not want to be around people who are happy. This makes for a strangely combative situation. Happy people struggle with maintaining happiness by simply existing in a world where many people do not want or appreciate their spirit.

This book is written with the hope not only you, the reader, will be happier, but that it ignites a happiness revolution,

We all know it is easier to remain happy around happy people. I encourage you to read this book. Learn the principles, and, then, share the gift with another. Or better yet, share the gift with a thousand others.

Let's make the whole world a happier place.

You Want This Book If...

- You have met me and wonder how I stay so positive ALL THE TIME.
- You want to be happier in general and find pleasure in the smaller things.
- You want to be able to survive in an environment inundated with negativity and still go home the happy person you ordinarily would be.

1. Are You For Real?

Happiness is a choice. You can choose to be happy. There's going to be stress in life, but it's your choice whether you let it affect you or not. Valerie Bertinelli

For the majority of my adult life, I have been a bit of an outcast, even considered weird or strange. If I wasn't seen as weird or strange, I was looked at as being straight up fake. While others battle things like self-esteem or self-image, I have always been judged for something uniquely me — being 'too' happy.

I know what you are probably thinking, is there such a thing as 'too' happy? Well if there is, it is embodied in the human being I am. I have been referred to as: freakishly happy, excessively bubbly, and the champagne lady, to name, literally, just a few. Usually, it doesn't hurt my feelings. My thoughts have always been this. If all you have is my bubbliness to pick on than I must be pretty amazing. In fact, I walk away feeling terrific about myself. That being said, I have had my feelings hurt many, many times by individuals who are cruel to me simply because they do not understand my particular brand of joy.

I learned long ago unhappy people do not appreciate happy people, or the Happies, as I like to call us. Rather, they find us annoying and strange. These "Anti-Happies" avoid us when they can and belittle us behind our backs. They imitate our giggles and high-pitched voices. They believe happiness and stupidity are one in the same.

I experienced this very phenomenon at a meeting once. I was bubbling over about something or other I had just learned. I paused when I realized another woman at the table was looking at me with an Anti-Happy glare. I stopped mid-sentence and looked at her expectedly.

I will never forget her words.

"You are a doctor? You seem more like a cheerleader than a doctor?"

I think I remember her words mostly because I have heard them a time or two before (more like 50!). Without skipping a beat, I gave her what has come to be my favorite response.

"I would be very careful equating happiness with stupidity. I truly would not want you to lead a miserable life." For the record, I do not believe cheerleaders are stupid, I just knew that was what she was hinting.

Suffice to say, I did not make a new friend, however, I was proud of myself for standing up for who I am. The truth is the Happies are everywhere and can be anything. We are doctors and lawyers, authors and actresses, moms and dads, and sons and daughters. Happiness is the one thing available to ALL people regardless of race, religion, socioeconomic status, or physical ability.

I have also frequently encountered people who adamantly and openly believe I am "fake" or "insincere." The one thing I can assure you of with perfect sincerity is what you see is what you get. I am not "fake" in any way, shape or form. In fact, if I were "fake" I would probably take it down a few notches in an effort to be more mainstream and fit in with much more ease - I don't see myself "going mainstream" any time soon.

This unique version of out casting has affected my life in many ways. I have been turned down for jobs, and told I seem uneducated (actually I have my doctorate, thank you very much!). I remember going on one particular job interview with the drug court program. While waiting for my turn to be interrogated, I noticed the subdued climate of the entire office. No one was loud, and I did not witness a single smile. There surely wasn't audible laughter or warm friendliness. I began to panic. I really wanted this job. The pay was more than double my current salary and there was a ton of upward mobility. Furthermore, it was downtown with an amazing view, and pretty much the job anyone would want.

When It was my turn to interview, I made the cognizant decision to "turn down the Chrissy factor" and become the person I believed they wanted for this position. I put on my glasses (the ones I only ever wear to drive because I am far too vain to wear them all the time), deepened and slowed down my voice and used as many fifty cent words as I possibly could.

And you know what, it worked! The interview was going famously, we were discussing offers and available offices when I realized what I had done. I had created this faux version of myself which WAS entirely "fake" and "insincere," and I knew I could not keep this up for years, months, weeks, or days, or even possibly hours.

I apologized to my interviewer and explained I was pretending to be what I thought they wanted and the real version of me would never fit in here. I allowed my voice to resume its regular happy tone, and the gentleman interviewing me just seemed disappointed. He had really wanted to hire the first girl he met, but the second seemed "too much like a cheerleader" to be a good fit.

I have struggled making and maintaining friendships because my happiness made them uncomfortable or uneasy. I have felt unwelcome in church groups and most social situations. I nearly always encounter someone who strongly dislikes me. I have actually begun groups and organizations and been run off because I make too many of them uncomfortable.

In one particular instance, my husband and I began a bible study together and invited several couples from church to join us. The first meeting went beautifully. We met at the park so the children could play while we enjoyed fellowship. We had such a great time we wound up getting dinner together afterwards. Unfortunately, the fun did not last.

The very next gathering left me feeling ostracized by the others, in a very deliberate fashion. They were all downloading a work out app on their phones so they could coordinate working out together, When I asked to join, I was told flat out no. No explanation. Just no followed by very loud silence. Unfortunately, my husband was guilty by association. The men were talking about planning a guy trip to Colorado at the very same meeting. When my husband attempted to insert himself in the conversation, he was told he was not invited. The next meeting was one I was never told about, and the meeting after that wound up being a confrontation about how my obvious "fakeness" made everyone uncomfortable. We were asked to leave the bible study group we created.

Despite this, plus a plethora of other stories, I continue to choose happiness. For me, the bright side far outweighs the dark. Sometimes I like to think of myself as a big ball of sunshine. Some people love to bask in it, others prefer the darkness because they do not like how sunshine illuminates their own shortfalls. I would like to believe that eventually the ball of light I am will help them find their way out of the darkness. Perhaps that is one of my biggest ambitions, being a light in a dark world.

Another reason I choose happiness is it is just plain fun. I know I am having more fun in my life than most people.

In one instance, my friends and I were riding the shuttle bus to the Tulsa State Fair. In our part of the world, the state fair is a pretty big deal. Some people save up all year for an Ultimate Ride Pass (permission to ride all the rides on every day of the fair) or even just to eat as much as possible (it is the only place I know where you experience such culinary delights as Krispy

Kreme cheeseburgers, deep fried gummy bears, bacon and caramel apples, and, my personal favorite, cricket pizza!). My friends and I are notorious for creating a ruckus anytime we are in public, and this fair outing was no exception.

The driver of the shuttle bus connecting us from a parking lot to a day of uncharted fun and food was playing an 80's music station, and it didn't take very long for our group to transform the bus into a karaoke party. I mean really, it was Michael Jackson's Smooth Criminal, who wouldn't be jamming?

The responses of the other riders were nothing short of fascinating. Some looked annoyed, rolling their eyes as dramatically as a 14-year old girl. Some were uncomfortable, shifting in their already uncomfortable school bus seats and avoiding anything even remotely resembling eye contact. The ones who intrigued me the most looked positively wistful. They saw the fun we were having, but something held them back and kept them from participating. Perhaps it was the people they were with or maybe they were just too embarrassed to be silly.

Maybe you are the wistful person on the shuttle bus to the fair. Maybe something is holding you back from the happy life you imagine. Whether its fear, embarrassment or peer pressure, something stops you from embracing those little moments in life making life more meaningful. If you are, please know this, the fun is worth it.

Having fun as a Happy does not stop at the state fair. For example, it is super fun to scare people. Really scare people. Maybe not in the sense of Jason Voorhees wielding a machete throughout the forests of Camp Crystal Lake – but believe me this bubbly girl can be downright terrifying.

One of my favorite preys of terror are the cashiers at Walmart, specifically the ones who look like they are having the worst day of their lives. I will literally go from checkout line to checkout line searching for, not the shortest line, but the one with the most obviously miserable cashier. I will quietly place my selections on the conveyor belt, while my husband and children try to find somewhere to hide - they know what is coming.

As the cashier begins her redundant process of beeping and bagging my groceries, I will wait for the perfect moment to loudly and happily say, "Hi!!! How are you today???" True story, I have startled some of them so much they have fallen over (this is hilarious, as long as they are not injured, then I would feel terrible).

They are always caught off guard and startled by my exuberance, and it usually takes a minute for the reality of what just happened to set in, but then the coolest thing happens. He or she will begin to smile and converse with me. We talk about anything– the weather, the horrible customer they had earlier in their shift, school, it really doesn't matter. What does matter is when I leave he or she is smiling. It made a difference. I made a difference. My wonderfully patient and loving husband will attest to this. I find great joy in scaring others with bubbly outbursts, but I find even greater joy in knowing I made their day a little bit happier than it was before they had the "Chrissy Experience."

It is also tremendous fun when random strangers ask me what I am on or if I am drunk. The truth is I don't need or want anything, in fact, I usually haven't even had caffeine! It's possible I have a hyperactivity diagnosis I don't know about, but who cares if I do? I have learned while happiness is not for everyone, it is definitely for me. It is far better than any drug, drink, or even coffee. I am simply having more fun and loving the life I have been given.

Now for the potentially surprising part…. I have not always been happy. When I meet new people, they always assume I was most popular girl, cheer captain, and prom queen; when in fact I spent the majority of my teen and early adult years quite the opposite. I suffered from depression long before it was a "thing"- and you could ask your doctor for a pill to feel better, I was bullied at school and struggled with my weight. I wore thick plastic glasses my classmates would call coke bottle glasses. I was called "psycho" because I cried so much. I was so sad, I literally could not hold it in.

Me in High School versus Me Now

These side by side comparison photos are fun to share because the people I am sharing them with are shocked, or in complete disbelief. In fact, many have argued with me about the legitimacy of these photos. In truth, it is amazing what age and eyeliner can do!

I have very few friends from this part of my life, namely high school and college. I was an extreme outcast, I remember my senior year in college, I was part of a music organization which hosted a Secret Santa party before the holiday break. As we were drawing names out of a hat, one of the guys in the group started freaking out and begging to trade. He was truly ugly about it, saying he would rather do anything than buy the person whose name he drew a present. I knew he had drawn my name. The Christmas party came and sure enough, I was the lucky recipient of his gift- a pair of cheap earrings from Wal-Mart. I left the party in tears and threw them away. The last thing I wanted or needed was a reminder of how much someone could dislike you for no reason at all. The truth is I hardly knew him, and he hardly knew me.

The friends I did have during this time are incredible because they loved me through the worst of me. Sometimes I wonder how they were able to do it. I was not easy to love. I definitely was not the fun-loving, pleasant woman I am now.

I am eternally grateful for them, and I hope you too are blessed by those who can love you when you cannot find the strength to love yourself. Two of these are no longer friends, they are my sisters.

My "Sisters," Suzie, Heather and me

Those years of my life were a literal nightmare, I considered suicide almost constantly, and even tried it once when I was 15. Obviously I did not die, but I did have kidney failure and was in the hospital for a long time. Little did I know at the time this whole incident just added more fuel to the fire for my bullies. Now they had this to make fun of me for as well. I was chubby, ugly, awkward, lonely and sad. I had friends who came and went, but I was never good at holding onto them.

I was not an innocent victim. During this time and beyond, I made a ton of bad choices, and realize I was to blame for many of my battles.

I was at my lowest when I decided since this problem was within me, so the solution must be within me as well. I think there is a lot of truth in the adage you have to hit rock bottom before things can get better. I know I did, and I know many others who had to hit rock bottom as well. Maybe you are at rock bottom, or dangerously close. If you are, I am glad you are reading this book. Please do not choose a permanent solution to a temporary problem. It can get better. I know because I lived it. I am thankful to be on the other side of what, at the time, was an insurmountable mountain. You can get here too.

I feel the need to offer a disclaimer here. Not everyone has the ability to make themselves happy. Some people struggle from chemical imbalances or other neurological impairments resulting in sadness, depression, and suicidal thoughts. If this is you, I encourage you to seek medical treatment. If however, you want to lead a happier existence, or you are on a good medication and therapy regime and want to jump in the rest of the way, this book is for you.

I clearly realize I had emotional issues which were outside of my control. Unfortunately, during my childhood mental illness and getting help for mental illness were just not "things you do." Historically speaking, during the same time, many individuals with serious mental illnesses were being "deinstitutionalized." In other words, huge psychiatric facilities were closing their doors and people were placed into community-based living. While this sounds like a wonderful thing, it had some downfalls.

Many of these individuals had never lived outside of an institution, at least not in a home they could remember. Many did not know who their families were, yet they were released with a Greyhound ticket to the last known address of their last known family member. Community living was a very new idea, and as most new ideas go, required a great amount of trial and error in regard to what works for these people and what does not.

Communities were in an uproar, most did not want people with mental health issues living in their neighborhood. They invented a term still used today when someone proposes the new construction of a prison, halfway house, or homeless shelter-NIMB - Not In My Backyard.

Conversely, many of these individuals behaved inappropriately, not out of malice, but rather out of ignorance and a lack of understanding societal rules and norms. Regardless of the intention, the general public grew increasingly afraid of something they did not understand–mental illness.

It could have been worse, I could have struggled during the days when the majority of the world believed mental illness was a demonic possession. If this had been the case, I would have had a hole drilled through my skull (to let the demons out) or been "Bloodletting" (allowing the demons to escape in a pool of blood).

This being said, stigma against mental health was a huge issue then and remains a huge issue in our nation today. People fear what they do not understand, and this fear is further exacerbated by Hollywood's depiction of mental illness, as well as the media coverage of mass shootings and other tragedies. I don't believe my parents wanted to deny me help. I don't think they knew how to help.

That being said, it has gotten better. There is far less stigma surrounding taking a mental health day at work or needing medication to feel less anxious or depressed. To the millennials and youngers, reading this book, do not be afraid to ask for help. There is no shame in needing it. Having problems in your brain is no different from having problems with your heart, your pancreas, or your liver. Do what you need to do to feel better.

I also cannot promise you will never have setbacks because you will. Life is like that—it just happens. People divorce, miscarry babies, lose jobs, lose friends, and bury parents. What I can promise is an overall happier life if when these setbacks occur, you have a strong mindset and a strong support system to get you through the rough stuff.

You will also reap a plethora of health benefits when you choose happiness. Research suggests happiness can result in:

- Lowered Blood Pressure
- Strengthened Immunity
- Alleviated Stress
- Reduced Aches and Pains
- Increased Life Expectancy

If all of this is not enough to convince you, research also suggests happiness prevents serious illnesses, including cancer, diabetes and heart disease. More commonly, happiness will even help you ward off the cold and flu. Simply put, happy is healthy.

I did it for myself, with the help of medication and therapy. I had legitimate mental health issues which needed to be addressed first, and I am not ashamed. I know I am not alone. I have faced the same struggles as millions of others. This is how I did it, and I find scientific literature supports my personal findings. So, if you are ready to become a "Happy," and see what "I am on," welcome to the happiness experience. May it transform your life.

2. Negativityland

When the negative thoughts come - and they will; they come to all of us - it's not enough to just not dwell on it... You've got to replace it with a positive thought. Joel Osteen

I know this one woman, we will call her Susan, who is a full-time resident of Negativityland. Susan saved loose change for years on end to go on a dream vacation to Paris. The moment her plane touched down on the tarmac, it began to rain. It poured the entire week she was there. Of course, in her world, this meant her entire trip was completely ruined.

Now, it's important to understand taking up residency in Negativityland means no matter how many good things happen to you, you will ALWAYS find fault in all of it.. Do you remember the character, Eeyore from Winnie the Pooh? This friend of Pooh Bear was a threadbare gray donkey who was always moping, depressed, talking to himself about the impending sadness and awaiting his inevitable tragedies.

Susan might as well be a gray donkey! This woman could win the lottery and spend the rest of her life perseverating on how it had ruined her life. No one ever leaves her alone! Everyone always wants more money from her! Do not get her started on the taxes!

When Susan came back from her vacation, she couldn't wait to tell me how everything had gone horribly wrong. I got comfortable. I allowed her to unleash her frustrations. I knew I was going to be exhausted at the end of this conversation.

For two hours she railed on about how horrible her vacation was and how long she had saved. She recounted every family member and friend she had ever encountered and how THEY got to have beautiful perfect vacations. This spiraled into everybody gets everything they want, and she gets nothing, ever. Nothing good ever happens to her. When will it ever be her turn?

In case you had any doubt whatsoever, the rain didn't ruin Susan's vacation. What really ruined her vacation was the inundation of negative thinking causing her to feel like a victim. It was her thoughts about the bad weather supporting an already overwhelmingly negative belief system and a preexisting bad attitude which ruined her trip. Let's be completely honest, most of us can have fun when it's raining.

When you allow circumstances outside of your control to determine your happiness, your natural state of peace deteriorates. When this happens, inner peace is replaced with a feeling you are being cheated. Everyone gets everything you want. The universe sucks and you will never win. Your inner peace is replaced by anger, resentment and hostility.

Peace and happiness are close cousins. Not the cousin you attempt to artfully dodge at the grocery store, but the one you actually like to hang out with. They fit together like puzzle pieces. The big picture doesn't make sense unless they are connected.

Think of your mind as the house of a hoarder. Stuff just crammed everywhere. In fact there is so much stuff it is difficult to move freely, and oftentimes you find yourself thinking how did I let it get so bad? If you are the type to blame others, you might look at your mess and say, "Why is life so unfair?"

Now imagine, perhaps with help, you clean up your hoarder home. You donate items you no longer need. You are now free to move. You can now live a more comfortable, happier life. This is peace.

When you realize you do not truly need all the unwarranted and unsolicited negativity [for some reason our brains love to hold on to with total desperation], you can achieve peace. This peacefulness will set you on the path to happiness.

When your brain goes down the rabbit hole of negativity, you reveal a lack of confidence in yourself and a failure to trust things can be good, even better than you imagine. As a result, everything you should be able to enjoy and appreciate becomes distorted, leaving you feeling like a victim and living an ultimately unhappy existence. You no longer have the confidence to make the necessary changes. You just continue to go deeper and deeper into the rabbit hole. The further you go, the worse you feel, and the more elusive true happiness becomes.

As much as they feel like they do, thoughts don't just happen. They are something we manifest and therefore logically should be able to control, at least to some extent.. They are the thoughts which imply ownership over "our" thoughts. When something bad happens, it is your thoughts about the situation, either minimizing or magnifying them, which determines the effect they will have on you.

Bad things happen to everyone, it is how you think about the occurrence and what you learn from the event which determines who we are at our very core. It is easy to feel sad or angry as the result of a bad or unjust occurrence. It is even harder to see the silver lining, and accept these moments as learning opportunities–a chance to grow.

It is relatively shocking I have not made a permanent move to Negativityland. For most of my life, and still really now, I believe I embody a walking version of Murphy's Law -the belief if something bad can happen, it will.

Several illustrations occurred in my early childhood. Anyone who knew my family, knows we loved, and still love going to amusement parks. Nothing was more fun than terrorizing my mom on a roller coaster or watching my dad drag a gigantic monkey through HersheyPark. All of this being said, if something could go wrong, it usually did.

On one particular outing at a small park in Altoona, Pennsylvania. we decided to take the paddle boats out onto the lake. My mom went with my sister, and I went with my dad. My mom and sister finished the loop, climbed out of their boat and waited patiently for us on the dock. And waited. And waited. And waited. Finally, my mom approached the ride attendant asking where we were. The ride attendant nervously laughed and told her he had accidentally put us on the broken paddle boat and were stranded on the lake.

Meanwhile, my dad and I were trying everything to get the boat going again. Paddling forwards and backwards, paddling with our hands, anything, but we were stuck. Park visitors began to gather on the bridge that went over the lake. One would think they would be sympathetic, but no. They pointed, laughed and took a whole lot of polaroids.

Fire trucks, ambulances, and police officers arrived on the scene to help the poor stranded father/daughter duo who clearly just did not know how to operate a paddle boat. Eventually the firefighters figured out a way to "fish us in" with an exceedingly long pole. I was never so happy to get off a boat in my life.

You would think at this point, I would have had enough of boats, but I think I might just be one of those people who truly never learns their lesson. Later that summer, at a different amusement park we once again chose a boat ride. This time I road with my mom thinking surely my poor father was the reason for the curse. I fell out! Of course, because I couldn't swim (another horribly embarrassing story) I needed to be rescued. Only to find out had I stood up, the water was less than two feet deep....

This Murphy's Law Curse continued into my adult life and continues today. Did you know blizzards in Las Vegas are very rare? The first one in 30 years hit in 2008, I know because I was there. Since Las Vegas was in the desert, I had prepared poorly, packing nothing but summer clothes for the entire trip. I have also been shopping in Branson, Missouri during a citywide power outage, and visited Hershey Park last summer when it was flooded. We never got any farther than Chocolate World.

One would think I should stop traveling, but the truth is this has not jaded me. In fact, I always tell friends and family 'traveling with me will be more memorable". Even if we are freezing in Vegas, we are still going to have a blast.

So, we can all agree bad things will happen and things do not always go according to best laid plans. What really matters is how we respond to the situation. Do we make the most of it, or do we choose to wallow in our own disappointment?

One of my favorite tricks when something bad happens is to imagine the most horrible worst case-scenario ever. This allows me to reframe what just happened within the context of "it could always be worse!" The truth is it can always be worse. For example, a blizzard in Vegas was not the worst thing in the world. In fact, some of the best activities in Vegas are indoors. Had the blizzard not happened, I may have had the opportunity to drink a Chocolate Coke at the World of Coke or ridden the rides in the Adventure Dome at Circus Circus.

Instead of ruminating about how bad things are and how bad things have been, make every attempt to make statements which cause you to see the situation in a positive light. Focus on the silver lining. What you will learn from this bad or unpleasant experience? How you will grow? The choice is yours. You can choose to become the victim or the victor. You can let the rain ruin Paris or you can find the rainbow, making even the worst scenario a memorable one.

I do not believe anyone is fully aware of how pervasive negative thinking truly is. I know I wasn't. Teenage Chrissy would spend hours looking in the mirror telling herself she was fat and ugly. No one has ever loved her. No one ever would. Eventually these thoughts would spiral until I was sobbing uncontrollably and wanting to die. My mother, to this day, reminds me of this horrific practice. She likes to point out how much love I have now. It was worth it to be where I am today.

Even if it is not extreme, if you pay attention to your thoughts, you will find you are not a positive person. Maybe you choose to tear yourself to shreds, second guess your decisions, or talk yourself out of amazing opportunities. Maybe you are negative towards others - criticizing them in your head, to make yourself feel like the more superior human being. I am guilty of that one too. Thoughts such as," at least I am thinner than HER," or "at least I am a better mom than HER" still creep into my thoughts - I squash them as soon as I recognize them.

Negative thinking does not make you a bad human being. If we were honest with each other, we would more than likely discover we are doing the same thing as everyone else. We all have dark thoughts, we all judge others, we all compare. It is all part of the human experience. I like to tell my students if you stuck a suction cup to your forehead and broadcasted your darkest thoughts through the projector and onto a big screen, everyone would be afraid of you. The funny thing is they never disagree. In fact, sometimes they share how sinister their thoughts can truly be. It's interesting because it unifies the students with a common thread. We really aren't all that different. We can all be scary and dark, it's normal for all people. The one thing we do not have in common, however, is the awareness of these feelings and thoughts and how to use them in a way to make us a happier person.

Happy people are not the thinnest people, the prettiest people, the richest people, or the ones with the nicest cars, houses, shoes or purses. They are normal people like you and me. We choose to grab onto the happiness, and let the rest go. I can say this because I know it's true. I was thin once (feel free to gasp in amazement). When the Atkins craze was popular, I lost 120 pounds, going from a size 22 to a size 0. It made me a horrible human being. I became mean, self-centered and conceited. I lost a bunch of friends, and even family. I didn't even like myself anymore.

Everyone I talk to who has experienced a transformative weight loss tells me the same thing. They literally could not handle the newfound attention. It was addictive and changed their very character. The most powerful lesson I learned from losing weight is this: Being thin has nothing to do with happiness. In fact, I liked myself a whole lot more when I am a bit fluffier. Thin people can be happy, pretty people can be happy, and rich people can be happy. It is all about your mind, not your position in life, and DEFINITELY not what you look like.

You are probably reading this and thinking, easier said than done. Maybe it's not as bad as you think. Remember, it is about awareness. At the risk of sounding all new "agey," you need to be mindful. Mindfulness is a state of active, open attention on the present and an opportunity to refocus on what really matters. Pay attention to what you are thinking. Did you just look in the mirror and cut yourself down? STOP! Give yourself a compliment and move on. Are you being sucked into a heated political debate on Facebook? STOP! Log off, put your phone on the charger, and go spend time with the people you love.

I need to offer another disclaimer here. This is actually pretty hard. I have had people tell me throughout the years this practice feels so foreign and uncomfortable they almost immediately revert back to their old ways and start insulting themselves because it is more comfortable.

The truth is change is NEVER comfortable. Were you comfortable on the first day of college when you knew no one? Were you comfortable when you started a new job, once again surrounded by strangers? Were you comfortable in a new city where you didn't know how to get to the nearest grocery store? Of course not. This is not comfortable and is not designed to be. I can however promise you, this step alone will change your life for the better. Getting uncomfortable is one of the best things you can do for yourself.

If this step wasn't hard enough, now you must consider what is going on around you. You might have noticed the average human being is absolutely inundated with negativity. It is everywhere! We get it from our friends, social media, television, work, and school, literally everywhere! In order to clear the negativity from our heads, we will need to look at each arena of our lives and do some serious spring cleaning.

Our Relationships

The good life is built with good relationships. Robert J. Waldinger

It is vital to have a positive support system. It is even more crucial to have these people in place for when you experience a difficult time, which you will. There are many negative people in the world, and even worse there are those who literally drain your joy and all your energy. My pastor, Craig Groeschel, calls those special people "relational vampires."

Relational vampires will bring you down. They will be counterproductive in what you are trying to achieve. You know who these people are. They are the people who after a five minute conversation are completely exhausted and cannot figure out why. I am here to tell you as a functioning adult, you will need all the energy and joy you can get. Keeping these types of people in your life can literally and figuratively be hazardous to your health, and I strongly encourage you to consider what good they bring, if any.

I realize ending relationships can be difficult, especially as an adult, but please accept you will need positive people surrounding you. Maintaining draining relationships are futile. I promise there are people out there who will invigorate and recharge you. Those are the ones you need to seek out.

These personalities will be different for all people. What is important to remember is to acknowledge how you feel in another's presence, to determine if they are a good person for you or not.

It is a psychological fact you absorb the energy and character of those who surround you. I know it's true for me. For example, if I am around people who swear a lot, it is only a matter of time before I am dropping f-bombs twice per sentence - and my husband totally knows who I had lunch with this week. You probably have these people too, whether you are willing to admit it or not. They shape you into a version of yourself you may or may not like.

I encourage you to take a hard look at those you spend the most time with. Do they bring you up or do they tear you down? Do they have addiction issues or other problems you could possibly absorb? Do they make you a better person, encourage your marriage or relationship, or motivate you to be a better version of you?

Choose the people who you seek out after a bad day. The ones who "fix" you so to speak. People who bring you up when you are feeling down or truly take the time to listen when you need to be heard. The ones who feel like sunshine are its absolute best.

Then most importantly, foster these relationships. Make time for them, remember their birthdays and treat them like the valuable gems that they are.

Social Media

With social media, people share mostly their best moments. Don't feel like you're not doing enough when you see a mom posting about making applesauce after you bought it. Ha ha! It's fine! Just for raising a little human being, you should be commended. Vanessa Lachey

Social media is a virtual cesspool of negativity. I promise you any blood pressure problems I wind up developing in this life are a direct response to human rights fights on Facebook. However, political confrontations aren't the only things destroying your happiness on social media. One thing most of us fail to realize is other people are posting their highly filtered, highlight reels. Believe me, I know. I never post the pictures where I look chubby. I use a number of filters and slenderizing apps! If I ever go missing, they are going to be looking for Beyonce instead of me.

The biggest threat to our happiness, in regards to social media is comparison. Comparison is almost a default reaction when it comes to scrolling through our Facebook or Instagram feed. Sure, a certain friend may have a bigger house than you or just went on, yet another, amazing European adventure, but want they don't share is they have just taken out a 3rd mortgage on their dream home and have acquired credit card debt in the six digits.

I am not necessarily advocating for you to remove all social media from your life, I am, however, suggesting you reframe the things you are viewing, and the subsequent thoughts you are experiencing as you scroll through. When you find yourself being attacked by the infamous green-eyed monster, stop yourself. Be happy for them! If they are on your "friends" list, then you hopefully like them (if not, may I recommend at least hiding them from your feed?), so it shouldn't be hard to be sincerely happy for someone you love. Remember, you have your own blessings to be thankful for, they just might come in a different flavor than their blessings.

We all have something unique. We all have a gift of our very own. Although we know this, it seems others will continue to inflict their value system on yours. I cannot begin to tell you how many people ask, "Now that you're a doctor, when are you going to buy a bigger house?" I simply do not need a huge house to brag about.. I love my neighborhood, and the best part is my house is almost completely paid off! I am thankful to be almost debt free. Buying a bigger house seems completely useless.

Try to remember these lessons when you are wasting time mindlessly scrolling through your social media. See the blessings in what you already have, not in what others think you should have, or things which makes you jealous.

Television

When you're young, you look at television and think, there's a conspiracy. The networks have conspired to dumb us down. But when you get a little older, you realize that's not true. The networks are in business to give people exactly what they want.
Steve Jobs

Have you watched the news recently? According to Peter H. Diamandis, the Chairman and CEO of the X Prize Foundation, 90% of the stories covered on American news today are negative in nature, and perhaps, even worse, it is because we, as Americans, like them better. Studies suggest Americans are far more likely to tune in to a negative story than a positive one. This resonates as truth for me.

I remember when 9-11 happened. Everyone was glued to their televisions watching the planes hit the World Trade Center over and over again. It was like we could not stop watching and waiting to see where the next plane would crash.

The Sandy Hook massacre was the same way. Everyone kept watching, despite the horror unfolding as more and more children were found. We do not watch television like this when the focus of the show is on puppies and babies. We will watch it once, smile, and change the channel.

As it turns out, we have a vast number of what are called cognitive biases. These cognitive biases keep us negative. We as human beings possess a negativity bias; the tendency to give far more attention to negative details than positive details. We also possess a confirmation bias, which is our tendency to selectively look at information or see information which confirms our preexisting notions. Which would be fine except our preexisting notions are typically negative and therefore we are confirming our negative expectations. In other words, we are already negative and choose to overwhelm our senses to keep us negative.

Horrifying, isn't it? Our brains are already hardwired for negativity and every time we turn on the television those neural pathways are strengthened, making us even more negative and less likely to blaze a new path towards positivity.

Think of your brain as a big forest. There are paths people have used for years and years. They are clear of debris and easily walkable. They have pretty views and have been enjoyed by many generations. These are the negativity pathways in your brain. They have been there for generations and have been used so much, they are easy to walk and clear of limbs and other obstacles.

Creating positive pathways would be the equivalent of getting off the path in the Amazon jungle. It's quite likely you are stepping somewhere which has never been trod by a human foot. It is hard. It is arduous. But then you see a beautiful flower which has never been seen by human eyes. Suddenly you realize blazing this new trail was totally worth it.

So, is it time to sell our televisions on EBay? Of course not, but it is important to understand this is how the brain works. If every time we turn on the news our brains are inundated with negativity, what can be done to keep negativity from controlling our lives?

Remember the good! For every bad thing you hear, instead of allowing it to depress you, replace it with something amazing in your life. Yes, it is tragic when lives are lost or crimes are committed. It is perfectly okay to stop and feel sad, maybe even pray for those affected (if you are the praying type). Remember how fortunate you are. It is not selfish to be grateful you and your loved one were not affected by something terrible affecting others. Use these very instances to refocus your energy on the amazing things happening in your own life. Be grateful. Remember to tell the people you love, you love them.

Work & School

One of the signs of a bad coworker is a pattern of persistent undermining - intentionally hindering a colleague's success, reputation, or relationships. Adam Grant

This one's a bit trickier. We all have a proverbial bad apple at work or school. The one who is unreasonably mean, or maybe over dramatic about everything! Some of my worst co-worker issues have been because of a "one-upper." For example, if my allergies were bothering me, they would be on the brink of death from hay fever. If my daughter was on the honor roll, they had children destined for Harvard or Princeton. We all know people who for some reason or another, we just don't click with. You will never be friends and will barely tolerate them throughout a particular job or work experience.

Am I telling you to drop out of school or quit your job? Of course not. For starters, you will find the exact same thing at your next job or school. You will simply never be everyone's cup of tea. Guess what? THAT IS OK! I have known people to become "job hoppers" because they kept encountering a bad apple at every job they had. No matter how hard I tried I could not get through to them that this was normal. You will never be liked by everyone, no matter how hard you try.

My suggestion is simple, in the words of a fellow "Happy," "FIND YOUR TRIBE!" Find those people who are positive and supportive, and if they make you laugh so hard you snort, even better! They are there, and if they are not in your office, it is OK too. You do not have to be friends with people at work. Your friends can be anywhere.

As for the others, ignore them, and if you can't ignore them, then kill them with kindness. In my experience, eventually you will grow on these people like a fungus. Sometimes they just need to see you are for real. You really are nice. You really are happy. You really are pleasant to be around. You may never become besties getting pedicures together, but you will tolerate each other, and sometimes tolerance turns into unexpected friendship.

3. Things Could Always be Worse

Gratitude can transform common days into thanksgivings, turn routine jobs into joy, and change ordinary opportunities into blessings. William Arthur Ward

It was another overly dramatic Friday evening at the Hiborik house.

"Nobody likes me!" I proclaimed loudly and with great anguish, as my mom tried to comfort me for about the 500th time this particular school year. It was another Friday night in which I hadn't been invited to the movies, to the mall, to a sleepover, or to a party, and, as usual, I was taking it horribly hard. This was a normal, routine part of my existence, and I would be lying, if it didn't still cross my mind as I am now approaching 40. Yes, sometimes I still believe nobody likes me.

Somehow when I was sad then, and even now, one of the quickest things I forget is how many people truly do love me. In high school, the truth is, I did not have very many friends, really very few, but I did have people who loved me then and who love me now. My oldest and dearest friend, Heather, was my Girl Scout camp pen-pal turned best friend. Heather would write to me nearly every single day. And, you know what, she loved me, in fact she still does. We don't write letters every day anymore, but we text every day, and we share every facet of our lives–weddings, kids, divorces, dramas, and happiness's. It's funny though because when I was sad then, and now too, I doubt that love, and let it escape my heart and mind. It is truly easier to forget our blessings than our hardships.

In society today, we are quick to forget the good things, and in turn focus on the bad. Research suggests Americans today are inescapably drawn to the negative, and not interested in the positive. We are comfortable in our misery. I always found this fascinating. No one went to kindergarten, sitting crisscross applesauce on the carpet, loudly sharing,

"When I grow up, I want to be the most miserable person ever!"

No one plans to be unhappy, it is just, more comfortable, to be unhappy. It is easier to remember what's bad, than focus on what's good.

If you think about your own life and the last conversation you had, whether on the phone, on the internet or in person, did you talk about the good stuff which was happening, or were you complaining? I am just as guilty. The last conversation I had today was with my husband, and I was complaining about the cold I cannot seem to shake. I complained about having to drive with tissues up my nose (cute, right?) because my nose was running so badly. I could have talked to him about the good things which were happening–the plans we made with the children this weekend, or the fun I was having getting ready for the holiday season. But, even from me, the happy girl, it was easier to remember how annoying my runny nose was then to refocus on the "good stuff."

So what would happen if we refocus our energy on embracing the good? One surefire way to refocus your energy on the good stuff is through the process of gratitude. There are many ways to show how grateful we are - the few suggestions I give are just that, suggestions.

- **Keep a gratitude journal.** Do not start a journal, write in it once or twice then leave it next to your bed to be swept under the bed by a feline passerby forcing said journal to live out eternity among the dust bunnies. You must commit to the journal. Start every day or end every day with writing a list of things for which you are grateful. Some days, many in fact, you will not feel like writing. Those days it will be hard to think of anything you are grateful for. Those are the days when you can feel free to be grateful for the air in your lungs, the fact you can see and hear, are not cold, hungry, or homeless. Be thankful for the spouse who is driving you absolutely insane? Somewhere someone is crying missing the spouse who has passed away. Those kids who just tie-dyed the cat? Somewhere a woman is crying because she just had another miscarriage. I hate to use the old adage of, "things could be worse," but the truth is they can be. All around you people are struggling with sickness, divorce and death. There are children living in impoverished communities making and eating dirt cookies. Your troubles may seem terrible and debilitating to you, but somewhere, someone else is thinking you are the luckiest person alive.

- **Do Some Cognitive Restructuring**. Cognitive restructuring is a useful technique for not only understanding unhappy feelings and moods, but also gives us the ability to challenge the sometimes-wrong "automatic beliefs" that can lie behind them. As such, you can use it to reframe, or restructure the unnecessary negative thinking we all experience from time to time. Some of us more than others. What does this have to do with being grateful? Sometimes all it takes is a simple rephrase of the negativity our inner voice is spewing to make ourselves grateful instead of irritated. Maybe an example will help. We all have a colleague at work or school just like the one I talked about earlier. We usually don't understand why said bad apple doesn't like us. In fact, he or she probably has never flat out told us they don't, unless they are super hateful. Usually we just feel someone doesn't like us or are annoyed by us. Words are never really needed. We know, and they know. One of my personal apples was always negative, I actually used to call her the Anti-Chrissy. She was a fountain of doom and despair level of negativity, so naturally we clashed. I remember one instance where she sent an email about me to everyone but me. Of course, I saw it. In fact, it was forwarded to me by nearly everyone else. I started to get my usual brand of upset, quickly reverting to my old school, "no one likes me!" verbiage. This time, I caught myself and choose gratitude instead. I reminded myself of the woman I met working at Dollar General. Like me, she had a PhD. Unlike me, she could not find a job in academia or in her field, so she was managing a Dollar General. I told myself, I bet she would tolerate 25 bad apples to be teaching at a university. I remembered to be grateful. The job wound up being a stepping stone to the job I have now, which is my dream job (I truly love my school!). I only had to survive one truly bad apple. I now have a whole bushel of colleagues who think I am funny, smart, and sweet. Needless to say, I did not lose any sleep that night. In fact, I fell asleep feeling pity for her. What a sad existence to have to hurt other people to make yourself feel like a better human being.

- **Connections**. If there is one thing in life to be grateful about, it is human connection. If you have heard me speak at a conference or have been my student, you will often hear me say connection is the cure for everything which ails us. It is the cure for depression and chemical abuse, it is the cure for loneliness and anxiety. It is the one thing which will help us feel better. Maybe more importantly, the lack of it, can bring us immeasurable unhappiness.

Sebastian Junger, a prominent researcher in PTSD, believes PTSD is less about the trauma of war, but more about the lost brotherhood [connection] upon coming home. He believes modern society causes anxiety and depression. True connection is the answer. There is safety in togetherness.

Imagine you had a circle of friends who truly protected each other, to the point of dying for each other. You would never doubt if you were loved or accepted because, for the only time in your life, you knew and fully believed you were. Together you experienced immeasurable hardship. You watched people die. Sometimes, you were the one responsible for the death. Through all the death and trauma, your circle loved and protected you. Then suddenly, you find your time is up. You are separated from this circle. Perhaps you are sent to a completely different corner of the world. You find yourself in a new community, perhaps a community you knew once but has now become foreign and unfamiliar. You are alone, without your circle for love, support and protection. Yes, there are people there who care about you, but it is not the same. They do not completely understand what you have seen or experienced. You, realize, how it feels to be truly isolated.

If you really think about it, you know deep in your heart Sebastian is right. Most people in present day American society feel alone and misunderstood. This feeling extends far beyond the traumas of war. It is everyone. We are immersed in a society trapped behind a pane of glass in the palm of our hands. We are incessantly comparing ourselves to the highlight reel shared by our supposed friends and followers. Without knowing the truth behind these Snapchat stories, we are scrutinizing ourselves against filters and unrealistic expectations. For many people, these are their only "friends." They do not understand us. They certainly would never die for us.

The friends to be grateful for in your life are the true friends. The ones who come over to cry with you when your dog has to be put to sleep or your spouse asks for a separation. The ones who, when you spend those precious moments together, wind up making you laugh so hard your throat hurts for the next three days. These friends know you don't always clean your bathroom and could care less if you never lose the baby weight. The ones who know they can show up without an invitation and aren't afraid to ask you to pay for some Starbucks and bring it to them, because they know you love doing it.

It's about genuine connection. Without it our likelihood for happiness drops significantly. You must find your people, nourish those relationships, form genuine connections, and be grateful for those connections.

I am very fortunate in this department. I have the best friends and family a woman could ever ask for; when I cry they cry. They make me laugh so hard I completely forget about the heartaches or stress currently snaking their ways into my happy existence. You need these friends. I promise they will make you happier.

My Best Friends and Me (Genie, Michelle, Rachel, Naomi and me)

I realize finding genuine connections gets harder with every passing year. When we were kids on the playground it was super easy to ask a stranger if they want to swing with us. Less than ten minutes later we would decide we were best friends. Adulthood is not the same. Even if you do have "friends," we all tend to get wrapped up in our own narratives. We are too busy with way too many children's activity (because making sure Bobby participates in soccer, t-ball, cub scouts, and violin lessons is the single most important thing ever), spouses, jobs, and of course, the God forsaken smartphone.

The truth is you could have made friends at the playground if everyone's nose wasn't glued to the screen as their children played. Potential friends are still all around you, just like when we were children. If befriending other parents at the park doesn't appeal to you, join a group at church, volunteer for an event or organization, join a club…. The opportunities are limitless, but it has to be a priority to not only make these connections but nourish them as well.

One suggestion to nourishing these important relationships: schedule it! Between Bobby's lessons, on Tuesday evening, meet at Starbucks. Have a lunch date every Wednesday. Enroll your daughters in the same dance class so you always have an hour together every week to strengthen your connection. I do this with my bestie, Michelle. Now I cannot imagine giving up Monday night dance class.

It must be a choice. You must make the decision to develop friendships and nurture them. It is so much easier to stay stuck in your own narrative, spending countless hours staring at a small screen. It gives you plenty of time for Netflix and naps (both of which are great), but there is absolutely nothing better than genuine connections and real friends. Both for the times when you need someone to laugh with and for the times when you cannot handle crying alone.

Finally, it is really important to keep gratitude fresh and new. If you start a gratitude journal and start writing what you are thankful for each and every day, eventually, like everything, it will get boring. It is crucial to find new and inventive ways to appreciate the life you were given.

You can express gratitude through art. Take photos of the things you are most grateful for. If you are artistically inclined, draw sketches or paint watercolors. You can sculpt or make collages. Regardless of your artistic medium, keep what you appreciate most in the forefront of your mind. Allow gratitude to be your muse and guide.

You can also express gratitude directly by talking to the people in your life. Tell them what they are doing well. Tell them how much it matters to you. I can promise their smile alone will make you a happier person and improve even the worst day.

Lastly, practice spontaneous gratitude. If you are having a down day or feeling especially stressed out, send an email expressing your gratitude to your supervisor or a favorite colleague. Not only does it help you, but it will also help them. Chances are if you are stressed at work, everyone else is too. Why not lighten everyone's load by showing some appreciation and kindness!

Gratitude is a struggle for many. Some people feel uncomfortable or weird expressing appreciation. I encourage you to not give up. Like everything, change is uncomfortable, but gratitude is the one gift which is not only a gift for you, but a gift for everyone around you.

4. Dumped on My Birthday

Optimism is the faith that leads to achievement. Nothing can be done without hope and confidence. Helen Keller

Hope may be the most difficult topic to approach when combining it with the search for happiness. Hope can sometimes be very difficult to find and even harder to hold onto. As citizens of planet Earth, we are thrown roadblock after roadblock while in pursuit of what we believe will ultimately make us happy. Often times we get there. We get the thing we thought we wanted so much only to discover it didn't make us nearly as happy as we thought it would. And then once again, hope is lost. We will never truly be happy. Happiness is a myth and an unattainable dream. It was never intended for someone like us, maybe not for anyone.

The first thing we need to realize when discussing hope is accepting the realization a "thing" will never bring us true happiness. In my life I have met people who placed every ounce of hope into one "thing." I can assure you happiness does not work like that. Maybe it's the dream house you always wanted. Perhaps you have drawn blueprints and picked out paint colors. You just know once you have built and moved into this dream house you will finally be happy.

Maybe it's a dream vacation. I, for one, border on being obsessed with seeing Paris. I think a big part of me already knows when I get there I am probably going to be disappointed, at least on some level. I see the Eiffel Tower, go on a catacombs tour, then look around and think now what? This has happened to me before, I get so excited and captivated with going somewhere. Even though it's wonderful,, I find myself thinking, "now what?" at the end or even halfway through the experience I had dreamed about for so long.

The same thing happened with my PhD. Of course, I was excited and thrilled the day I defended my dissertation. I had friends who had earned PhDs before me, and they had been so adamant when they told me there is absolutely nothing better than hearing, "Congratulations, Dr. Whiting!" for the first time. This is absolutely true. It felt terrific! However, a few minutes later on the drive home from Fayetteville, Arkansas with two of my best friends I began to wonder, "Now what?" The joy and excitement was short lived, because I honestly had no idea what was going to happen next.

I am not saying to not be hopeful about things. Things are wonderful! We all want a home, a car, and the ability to make treasured memories. I am saying when you are placing all your happiness in the procurement of a possession the joy will be short-lived. True happiness rests in eternal hope, not stuff. So, when you find yourself, saying anything like, "Once we move out of this cramped apartment, I will finally be happy," catch yourself, and refocus your hope on the things which truly matter.

So, what does matter? What is eternal hope?

Deep within the core of hope is the belief things can change. No matter how awful or uncertain they are, things can turn out better. Possibilities exist. Hope sustains you. It keeps you from collapsing into despair. It motivates you to tap into your own capabilities and inventiveness to turn things around. It inspires you to plan for a better future, not only for you but for everyone.

Have you ever met, [or maybe you are], a person who only sees the bad in the world? They watch the news every night and fixate on the hard facts. More people are dying. More people are starving. More people are struggling than ever before. The truth is this. It has been bad before. It will be bad again.

Historically speaking, we, as a human race, have always been compelled to hate or persecute someone or something. In the 1840's, over one million people in Ireland starved to death, during the Irish Potato Famine. Another million emigrated from Ireland hoping for a chance to live. During the famine many called a genocide, Ireland was under the rule of Great Britain, which means at any point, the British government could have stepped in and helped them. They didn't. This event was a watershed moment in Irish history because it decreased the population of Ireland by 25% and started a revolutionary movement in that nation.

The most tragic part of the famine was the realization help could have been given, but it was withheld. Why? I obviously wasn't there, but I can assume it was because they hated them. Much like politics today. Refugees are turned away, and wars are fought over hate no one truly understands. Why would anyone hate another human being simply because of where they were born, the color of their skin, or the God they worship? All of this remains a mystery to me. However, in the case of the famine, things did get better. I don't live in Ireland, so I can't really say if the hate is still there. I do know things have gotten better because mass groups of people are no longer slowly starving to death.

This is only one example of times in our planet's history where things were so catastrophic, hope was lost for many. In the 1940's Adolf Hitler and the Nazi Regime ordered the genocide of not only the Jewish people, but anyone else they deemed "undesirable." An estimated 5.9 million Jews died during this atrocity, along with over 150,000 disabled people, and a still unknown number of gay people.

These, along with many others were times in our horrific history when all hope was lost. However, hope did come back, the Irish continue to live and prosper, and the Nazi regime fell from power during World War II. While hope for many had been lost during these terrible times, hope in humanity was restored for others.

Without hope, we have no happiness or joy, but how do we discover hope when all hope seems lost? How can we change our perspective to embrace the mindset things can and will get better? Most of us have been in a dark place where all hope seemed lost, and, in my opinion, it is the single hardest place to escape from. This is when suicides happen and addictions takes over. It feels like a dark hole with no ladder to climb out and no light in sight.

When I was working on my Masters' degree at Langston University, I took a class about addictions in which we were required to attend 12 step meetings and write reflection papers on our experiences. I began this assignment with dread in my heart. I fully expected to feel uncomfortable and out of place, but, surprisingly the complete opposite happened. The people I met through these meetings were incredible. They simply radiated hope and encouragement. What a wonderful experience for these individuals! They had lost all hope and turned to substances for an escape from their dark hole of despair. Yet here they were! Being a light for others! I fell in love with the 12- step program! It is all about hope, and not just hope. It is about hope for everyone. No one is too deep in hopelessness to have a chance for happiness.

One of my favorite things about the 12- step program is the slogans they teach to the individuals attending the meetings. They are short little phrases designed to serve as reminders. Not all is lost. Some of the catchphrases I continue to use today:

- One day at a time. You do not have to try to be clairvoyant, but you can live each day to the fullest, and live it as happily as possible. Forget the past, forget the future, embrace today. It will get better, one day at a time.

- This too shall pass. When I lost my daughter, Claire, I remember believing I would never be me again. I stayed in bed for weeks, crying, and begging God to change what had happened. I prayed to wake up and discover it was only a terrible nightmare and Claire was still here. Anyone who has experienced a miscarriage or lost a child knows and relates to what I am talking about. I thought I would never smile again and never laugh again. I believed the old Chrissy who laughed and smiled, and most people thought was on drugs (kidding, kinda) was gone forever. She was simply dead. However, what they say is true, time does heal. I still think about Claire every single day. I talk to her and imagine what she would be like today as a boisterous preteen. However, I have also re-embraced my own life, as well as the life of my other amazing daughter, Carina. And, I have become "me" again.

- Your worth should never depend on another person's opinion. This one may be the most important. Never let another individual dictate what your future holds and for what you should, or should not, have hope. When I was in high school, I had a guidance counselor who told me I was "too crazy" to go to college. He would not help me with applications or on any college preparation. Thankfully, my school had a second guidance counselor who was a godsend. She helped me with the process to, not only be accepted, but get a scholarship to my first- choice school. My advisor was incredible– helping me with financial aid and ultimately turning my dream of a college degree into a reality.

This is the point where you need to realize hope belongs entirely to you, and no one has an opinion that matters. Did I let the first guidance counselor stop me from later becoming a doctor? Heck no! I allowed his hate to fuel my fire! His treatment of me isn't the only time I allowed the naysayers to fuel me, it has been an almost constant in my life. I have had so many people throughout the years tell me I wasn't good enough. I wasn't smart enough. I wasn't creative enough. I wasn't thin enough. I wasn't pretty enough. None of this was true. And it's not true for you either. You are more than enough. You are amazing! And tomorrow is going to be better than today! I promise, it will get better!

It makes me positively ill to think about how one person's voice can destroy another person's hopes and dreams. Remember this, misery loves company. There are people in this world who are dying to pull you down to their level or lower - so they can feel better about themselves. Do not let these people control your life or dictate your outcomes. You can pity these people, but do not let them control you! You are the creator of your own destiny and the artist of your own masterpiece. So, what if someone doesn't like you or thinks you can't do something! Chances are for every "Unhappy" you have in your life, you have ten cheerleaders in your corner, rooting for you, loving you, and supporting you. Tune the other noise out!

Still struggling? Perhaps it is time for a reality check. One of the tricks I like to do is to check myself. I love the expression, "Check Yourself, Before You Wreck Yourself." Remember you are the master of your destiny! When I feel myself starting to get upset, which does happen, contrary to popular belief. I stop myself and ask myself this question:

"Will this matter tomorrow? Will this matter next week? Next month?"

It is positively shocking how often the answer is no, it doesn't. Armed with this knowledge, I am able to shake it off, and move on with my life. It's easier to keep smiling and just keep swimming when you are fully aware, "this too shall pass". It is mind blowing how often we let stress and anxiety over the little stuff control our lives. You have to realize things will work themselves out. They always do.

I still get stressed, in fact, sometimes it seems like I have to jump more hurdles than most people over the simplest things. But, here's the truth, you either jump the hurdles or you take a different path, either way it will work itself out.

I am not saying life is always easy because it's not. In fact, there are times life can be downright cruel. Jobs are lost, divorces happen, people die, teenage children lose their minds—there will always be stress, there will always be sadness, there will always be frustration, but you alone have the choice of how you are going to respond to these situations; and have hope great things are right around the corner.

This is also probably an appropriate time to think about this. Without the negative you would never truly appreciate the positive. When people meet me, they quickly assume I have always been happy, bubbly, and optimistic, but the truth is my life has been far from perfect, complete with many disappointments and, at times, complete devastation. In hindsight, which of course we all know is 20/20, I see where these moments have manifested into something wonderful, or, at the very least, taught me an appreciation for when things are good.

For example, it's much easier to appreciate a marriage in which you are happy if you have had relationships which made you miserable. My husband is terrific about the little things. For example, if he stops to put gas in his car, he will always grab me a Coke (my favorite nemesis) and a snack. He doesn't ask, he just does it because he is thinking of me. I am not sure I would appreciate this gesture nearly as much as I do, had I not had relationships in the past where I was rarely thought of. I actually had a boyfriend in high school (ninth grade to be exact) who broke up with me on my birthday. He apologized for doing it on my birthday because he claimed he had no idea it was my birthday. According to him, he thought he was breaking up with me on some random day. Funny thing is my birthday falls on New Year's Eve One would think it would be easy to remember.

My husband, Matt, never forgets my birthday. However, without the darkness of being dumped on my birthday, I am not sure I would appreciate him as much as I do. It takes the bad to embrace the good.

My Sweet Husband, Matthew, and Me

One of my favorite stories of finding hope in the darkness comes from a dear friend of mine, who had to endure more than most can begin to imagine. Alan, as we will call him, was happily married to "Becky" for several years. I remember assuming they did not want children because they did not seem to be in any hurry to have them. In fact, I don't recall a single time early on in our friendship when they mentioned trying to conceive. As our friendship developed I learned it wasn't that they did not want children, they could not, or at least, were struggling to have children. Amazingly, after several rounds of in vitro, Becky became pregnant, and nine months later delivered a beautiful baby boy, "Justin."

It was truly a miracle baby, and I remember feeling so happy for them. Our families would spend time together, and for a time life was good. Sadly, the happiness did not last.

Justin was diagnosed with leukemia at two-and a-half. After a long and emotional battle, he died in Alan's arms at age seven. Alan, who had always been a Christian, plunged into a world of darkness and despair. He blamed God for taking his child from him and became angry and cold.

Alan completely lost his faith and eventually his marriage ended. I remember him telling me during this time he could not go out in public without becoming enraged. Something as simple as two girls giggling at the shopping mall, would send him into yet another angry spiral.

"How dare they!" He would say. "How dare they go on living as if nothing has happened?"

Since his whole world had stopped it was completely unfair for others to go on living. Since he was sad, it was unfair anyone else should be laughing. Everyone should have to experience the insurmountable pain he was experiencing.

It was one of these trips out to the real world, when his heart finally began to thaw. While waiting in line at Starbucks, he overheard a woman having a conversation with another woman about her age. She was telling her friend, or maybe sister, her doctor had given her 30 days to live. Her friend, or sister, responded with a simple, "How do you want to spend your last 30 days?"

Alan turned to look in their direction and saw the first woman who spoke had no hair. Obviously she had been battling a sickness similar to that of his son, and she too was losing the battle.

For reasons Alan still cannot fully understand, the woman with no hair profoundly affected him. What if he only had 30 days left? He would only have a month to go. Life is like that. Unlike the woman at Starbucks, most of us never really know when our time is up.

Alan decided in that moment he did not want to spend what could just as easily be his last 30 days on earth being infuriated at those who dared to show happiness in his presence. In fact, it was then he realized this is not how his son would want him to live. Justin, throughout his entire ordeal, had always stayed happy and upbeat. He surely would want the same for his father.

It was a slow and sometimes painful process, but Alan found hope again. He found hope, first as a hospice volunteer, where he quickly learned how much these families and patients needed someone like him. They needed someone who had lived through it, and could relate, at least on some level. Alan explained it like this:

"Many people who know their time on earth is coming to an end do not want to talk to their family and loved ones about what they were experiencing. They already feel like a burden to their loved ones in regard to medical care. Caregivers are also burdened with knowing the one they love will soon be gone."

Alan became important to these people. He became the person they could talk to about their fears of death, the guilt of being the cause of so much sadness, and anything else they needed to express. He was there for them at a time of suffering, perhaps when they needed someone the most.

Alan discovered he loved helping others and wanted more. He returned to school and received a master's degree, along with a counseling license. He is now remarried and living a very happy life. He thinks about Justin every single day, and still misses him. He wonders what he would be like as a young adult today. Perhaps, the most powerful message in Alan's story is without knowing and loving Justin, he would have never found his passions in life. So many people would never have been helped. To everything there is a purpose, and without Justin's story, many people would never have had the gift of Alan.

Without hope, happiness will always remain elusive. I have been in the pit of despair and wouldn't wish it on my worst enemy. While searching for happiness, you must find hope. Real hope. Hope in humanity. Hope for this world. Remember things, although they provide temporary joy, are not forever. True happiness is believing in happiness for others and spreading joy to the world. Gandhi said it best, "Be the change you want to see in the world." Be the one who lights up the lives of others, because true happiness is finding happiness for others.

5. A World Without Peanut Butter Cups

The true secret of happiness lies in taking a genuine interest in all the details of daily life. William Morris

Is there anything better than something new?

Something new can attract our attention and interest creating not only excitement and joy, but fueling our motivation as well. We become ready to bring energy and focus to the task at hand. We are inspired by new possibilities and want to learn where they will lead. In the workplace, when we are assigned to a new job, or forced by circumstances to look for a new one, we are faced with new challenges. These challenges bring opportunities to learn new skills—skills which otherwise might not have been learned - had the job changes not occurred. We feel ready to tap into this inner motivation and achieve the sense of excitement and purpose people feel when they are thoroughly involved in their jobs.

These can also be the scariest times in our lives, when we become completely inundated with negative thoughts and self-doubt. Our brains are not necessarily wired in the best possible way. Self sabotage and second guessing come naturally to most of us. At least more naturally than strength and confidence do.

One of the very scariest days of my life was the first day of my doctoral program at the University of Arkansas in Fayetteville, Arkansas. I was, once again, thrust into the throes of being the teenage girl who was not smart enough or stable enough for a college degree, but here I stood, attempting a doctorate from a huge, prestigious university. I seriously felt like I was 15 again–chubby, awkward, and simply not enough to achieve what I was about to attempt.

My fears were not completely unjustified. Again, I found myself in a situation where I did not fit in, and most of the people around me believed I was either really weird or just a total fake. Since I was a two hour [each way] commuter student, I didn't have the opportunity to bond with the people in my cohort. They were left to fill in the gaps of what I was really like. I would love to say it got easier and I developed beautiful lifelong friendships, but that simply was not the case. I think the saddest part was that I actually liked all of them. They were all smart and had so much to contribute. I remember wishing I was as smart as they were. It all seemed to come so easily to everyone else.

It was not easy. The coursework was hard, really hard, especially statistics. I have always been one of those people who has never been good at math. I realize I have created a self-fulfilling prophecy, but the fact remains I have struggled with every math class since fractions in 4th grade. Since I did have the dreaded two-hour commute each way, I had lots of opportunity to cry my eyes out in peace. Sometimes out of pure frustration, and other times out of fear I had started something I would never be able to finish. Sometimes it was because my classmates believed horrible things about me. To this day, I do not know how any of those rumors started..

But, you know what, I did it. I am a doctor. I overcame all the odds and went all the way. I wrote and defended a dissertation, all while being a single mother. If I had given up, I wouldn't be where I am now. I get to teach psychology at a wonderful institution and have a life I truly love. I love my students and my colleagues. I am lucky to have landed in such a great place. I wouldn't be where I am now if I hadn't been inspired to become a college professor, first in my undergraduate experience at Saint Vincent College in Latrobe, Pennsylvania where I had the most incredible professors - Dr. Slank-Montemurro, Father Rene Kollar, Father Vernon Holtz, and Father Mark Gruber, to name just a few. My teachers there were incredible and so passionate about what they were teaching, I wanted to be just like them. My Masters program at Langston University simply relit the fire. My professors there were equally passionate and incredible–Dr. Sassin, Dr. Quinn, Dr. Sanders and Dr. Lewis were all so encouraging. I really began to believe I could go all the way in my education.

Me Receiving My Doctorate

I wouldn't be where I am now if I hadn't become fascinated with both psychology and rehabilitation. Honestly, I can't understand why everyone does not become enamored with these fields. I want to know why some people become cannibals and others cannot stay out of casinos. I want to know what it takes to rehabilitate an individual who has just been to Hell and back. I want to change the world and inspire my students to do the same. I want them to do great and amazing things, so I can sit on my couch in my comfy pants watching the news and remember when they were my student.

I certainly would not be where I am today if I had listened to all my own negative self-talk. I would love to say during this entire adventure, I looked in the mirror, and said, "You got this, Girl!" But the truth is, I had to fight myself every step of the way. I cried, a lot. I thought about quitting, a lot. I felt stupid, a lot. My family and friends always say I made it look easy, but the truth is it was really, really hard. What got me through was inspiration. I was inspired by my mentors, and later my students. In fact, they still inspire me to grow, learn, and be a better version of myself. I am really proud of myself. I wish I could say the entire experience was a happy journey but it wasn't. The reality is I am happier because of it.

It is important to remember every journey is not a pleasant one. Life can be hard. Life can be cruel. These are the moments defining who we are, refining us in fire. I have experienced many moments in my 40 years where I thought I could not get through, but I did. You will too. There is always another, brighter side in every struggle.

So what interests you? What inspires you? When do you feel the most proud of? I fully understand not all of you want to become doctors or CEOs of your own company. For you it could be so much simpler. Maybe your dream is to find love and become a terrific spouse (I, for one, love being a wife!).

Maybe you can't wait to have children and have always dreamed about being a mom or a dad (I love being a momma too!). Maybe you long to be an amazing bargain hunter or coupon queen. The possibilities truly are as endless as your imagination. Only you know what fuels your fire.

The secret is this. You need to remember these things when you are on a difficult journey or even just having a bad day. One of my favorite professors during my doctoral program would always remind me to keep my eyes on the prize. Sometimes the road to happiness is a bumpy one, and sometimes it is downright treacherous. However, if your path is inspired, you will overcome. You will persevere. You will accomplish your goal. Perhaps most importantly, you will be happier because of it.

You will find your inspirations and ambitions will change as you age and grow. If you find yourself, "in a rut," as my mother calls it, it may be time to discover new interests, inspirations, and something to be proud of. It may be time to light a new fire and begin a new path. You are never too old to reinvent yourself. In fact, it is inevitable. In my future, I hope to be reinvented as a successful self-help author and someday, but not too soon, a grandmother.

Maybe you are bored. People who are bored will sometimes do things considered horrifying to others. Perhaps you start an affair or pick up a bad habit-like drugs, alcohol or gambling. If you are bored, or "in a rut" rather than turning to things which may end in destruction consider finding a new inspiration. Maybe it is time for a career change or to go back to school. Maybe it's time to start that business, blog or YouTube channel you have been thinking about. With new inspiration, comes good feelings like creativity and motivation. It makes you feel happy again.

I remember finishing my PhD and thinking, "Now what?" I almost felt lost. Yes, I was proud, but at the same time, I felt done. I had to find new ways to feel inspired and new interests. I am inspired by my students and the people I meet when I am speaking at conferences. They all challenge me to be a better version of myself. I am at a point in my life that instead of asking, "Now what?" I ask, "What's next?" This book is a perfect example. I loved sharing my thoughts on Positive Psychology and how to be happy with my students and conference attendees.. My natural "Now what?" was to write a book and hopefully reach more people. Instead of allowing myself to fall into a rut of just teaching and conferences (although I completely love these things), I allowed the people in my life to inspire me to take it to the next level.

Allow the people in your life to give ideas, ask for suggestions and accept the criticism. Ignore the Anti-Happies. Realize there will be people who are jealous of you. Those who want nothing more than to tear you down.

If you don't have anyone in your life who does this for you, it may be time re-evaluate your support system and your social network. Remember, you ultimately become the people you choose to associate with, and I don't know about you, but I would like to think I inspire others to do incredible things. You do not want to associate with people who don't believe in you and fail to encourage you to be a better version of yourself.

One of my very best friends is an artist - a legitimate, makes a living from it, artist. She is simply incredible and amazingly talented. I used to tease her. I would say I was so jealous that she had such a marketable talent, and all I had was being excessively happy. She would tease me back and say being excessively happy was totally marketable. Turns out she was right. I have made a career out of being happy and sharing happiness with others.

A few years ago, my best friend made the difficult decision to re-evaluate her support system. It was a very difficult and painful process which resulted in her asking to take a break from certain individuals to work on her marriage and herself. These friends chose to interpret her decision as a permanent arrangement resulting from her jealousy of their success.

The truth is these individuals were choosing to base their own success on whether or not my best friend was succeeding or failing, and it had become a very unhealthy dynamic for all of them. Instead of building her up, they would attack her for being jealous of their success. It was hurting my best friend deeply and causing her to second guess her own talents and capabilities. Since reassessing her support system, she has become enormously successful. She has been featured in art shows in different states. Most recently, she started a non-profit merging her love for the arts with mental illness awareness and anti-stigmatization.

Choose people who inspire you to be better, not those who tear you down. If you continue to surround yourself with negativity, eventually you will begin to believe it. You will fall into a rut and lose hope. These things all fit together, and without every ingredient, you will never get a chance to taste your own happiness cake. Chase the things fascinating you. Follow your dreams. Do not settle. If you get bored, find new interests. Chase new dreams, and still, never, ever settle.

What if you don't know what interests you? May I suggest an interest inventory? O-NET offers an amazing one. It is absolutely free at mynextmove.org. Regardless of which inventory you choose, it is imperative to not think about money while you are answering the questions. Money is one of those "things" we talked about. It will never lead to lasting happiness. Another of my favorite expressions is if you are doing a job you love, you will never work a day in your life. As for finances, in my experience things always find a way of working themselves out. Have some faith. Embrace what truly makes you happy. You can do this.

What if it doesn't work out? Keep trying! Persistence always pays off. If you know this is your path, then stay the course. Some of the most successful people I know, failed the first time. Milton Hershey, the creator of the world's most beloved candy, went bankrupt twice before becoming the success he is known for today. First he failed at a caramel company in Philadelphia, then he failed at a second attempt in New York City. It wasn't until he paired his knowledge with chocolate in his third attempt did he ultimately found success. Had he given up after his first, or even second failure, we wouldn't have peanut butter cups today. He knew what held his interest and passion, so he kept trying.

The truth is he knew what he wanted and never gave up. Never give up on the path to happiness. It may hurt getting there, but in the end, it will all be worth it.

Milton Hershey stands as a role model for us in another way. Once he did achieve success, which he definitely did (you would be hard pressed to find someone who doesn't know what a Hershey bar is), he created an orphanage which provided impoverished boys with not only a school, but a curriculum designed to teach character and break the cycle of poverty. Each of these boys were taught trades and given a chance to continue with a college education.

Milton Hershey also saved many lives during the great depression by expanding production and creating jobs for those who had lost theirs in the recession. He gave tens of thousands of dollars to local churches to help families continuing to struggle.

Milton S. Hershey died with very little wealth and even fewer personal possessions. Near the end of his life he shared his own personal recipe for happiness,

"I never could see what happiness a rich man gets from contemplating a life of acquisition only, with a cold and legal distribution of his wealth after he passes away."

Hershey believed the secret to happiness was giving happiness to others and serves as a reminder: Things will never procure true happiness.

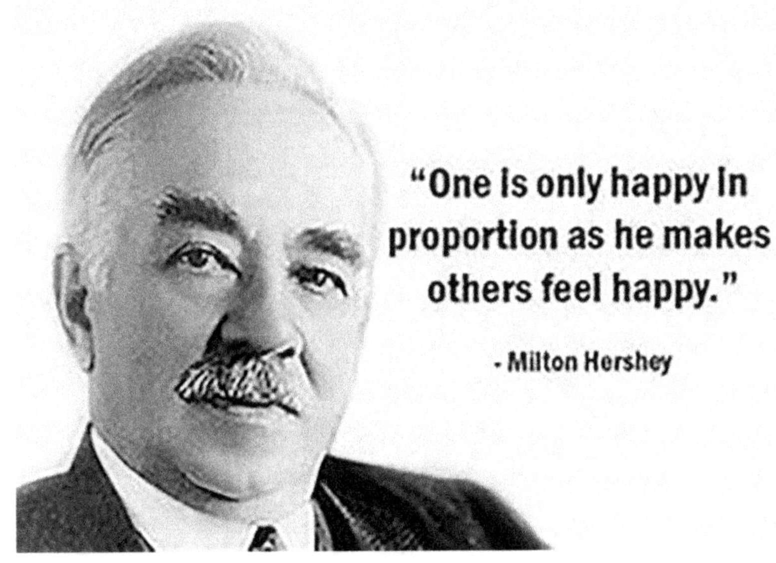

6. Throw Kindness Like Confetti

Let's not judge. Let's draw inspiration from each other's stories - successes and failures - and realize we're all connected. Cory Booker

Have you ever been the recipient of a random act of kindness? Maybe someone has paid for your coffee while you were in the drive thru of your favorite coffee shop or maybe someone paid for your meal when you weren't paying attention. Or maybe you were me. I had a wonderful random act of kindness not too terribly long ago. Funny thing is, it was exactly when I needed it the most.

Money was feeling particularly tight while I was working on my doctorate. I was a single mom and couldn't hold down a full- time job while commuting to Arkansas from Oklahoma. I made the drive at least twice a week, five days a week during the summer. I had a mortgage payment, tuition, and had chosen to make the commute in a 1997 Honda Civic, because it was economical, and I could not afford a car payment. In fact, the car was given to me by my artistic best friend's family, so I had a way to commute! I was so fortunate during my doctoral program to have so much love and support. Thank goodness for my mom during this time because I would have never made it without her. She helped financially, she paid my tuition and she took care of Carina, my daughter while I was a state away trying to create a better life for me and her. I was also precariously balancing several part time jobs to help as much as I could.

Of course, it was right before payday when a strange new light came on in my little green "junker". I was halfway between school and home. I had no idea what the light even meant. In a panic, I began to call every male I knew (sorry girls, I went there!) Thankfully, the car wasn't sputtering to its final death, it just needed an oil change; an oil change I could not afford. I continued the commute while watching the percentage numbers of the life left in my oil drop quicker than I felt they should.

Frustrated I pulled my car into my neighborhood automotive shop and went inside to request an oil change. I was in a very bad mood and completely exhausted after a full day of teaching classes, attending classes and of course, driving. The very friendly man at the counter greeted me warmly and offered his assistance. I swear he knew how obviously unhappy I was. He countered it beautifully. I remember asking for the "cheapest oil change he had because I was a teacher and a graduate student and money was tight." He smiled and set to work, while I sat in the lobby doing school work on my laptop. I was still crabby. I just wanted to go home, spend time with my daughter, eat, and sleep.

About 30 minutes passed, and my name was called. While fiddling in my purse for my wallet, the same gentleman smiled and handed me my keys.

"The cheapest oil change I have for a teacher is a free one", he said with a twinkle in his eye.

I couldn't believe my ears. I started insisting to pay. He gave me the same insistence right back. I felt happy, lucky, and maybe most importantly, inspired to do the same thing for someone else. I wanted to pay it forward. I wanted everyone on earth to experience the same incredible feeling I was feeling at that moment over and over again. The crabbiness was gone.

I ask the same question at my lectures,

"Have you ever been the recipient of a random act of kindness?"

I wish you could see the faces of my participants as they recall the same feeling I had experienced one evening in an automotive shop. What excites me the most, is how they all start to share stories of times it happened to them and they got to pay it forward to someone else. It always seems they enjoy giving the gift to someone else far more than they enjoyed being the recipient.

Listening to these strangers and students enthusiastically share their tales of "throwing kindness like confetti" gives me hope in humanity. What if everyone was doing this? Sharing this feeling? Living this way on a daily basis? What would the world be like?

Whenever you feel inspired to do something whether for yourself or for another person, know this. It will bring you happiness and joy. I have never regretted throwing kindness like confetti. You won't either. Sure, not everyone has the means to pay for someone else's meal, but you definitely have the capacity to make a difference in someone's day. If you see someone alone or struggling, give them a smile or a compliment. It's more than OK to tell someone you love their haircut or how impressed you are with their children's behavior.

Something I have learned on my short time on this planet, is to never deny someone else a blessing. Whether you are spiritual or not, you have more power in your words and actions than you can begin to comprehend.

Think about it. How good do you feel when you are out and about and some stranger walks up to you and tells you that you have the best hair or the most infectious smile? It feels AWESOME! Why would you ever keep this gift from someone else?

If you have something nice to say, say it. It might feel weird or awkward at first, but it won't with practice. This is what happens. You see someone, anyone doing something amazing, wearing something awesome, or with a breathtaking feature, walk up to them and you tell them. That's when the magic happens. As the individual begins to absorb what you are saying, their face will radiates a beautiful light, and the best part is you get to absorb the light too. You both get to walk away feeling great.

It will become addictive, the light I mean. It is far better than any drug (at least I assume). You will find yourself seeking out people to which you can throw your kindness confetti. It doesn't stop there. You will up your game even more. You will start to look for the people who need the light. The people who are sitting alone at the library or just look like they are having a bad day. You will use your new superpower to slowly change the world, or at least your sphere of influence. AND IT WILL MAKE YOU FEEL AMAZING.

It doesn't stop there either. Your behavior will inspire others to do the same thing. They will remember how your words or actions made them feel. They will want to gift the gift to someone else. Think of it as the ripple effect in a pond. You have tossed the first stone and now the ripples radiate out. They affect every other corner of the pond. It's a happiness revolution.

Inspiration can go farther than random acts of kindness. When you feel inspired to do something, you should always do it. Maybe you have been inspired to write a book or start a company. Maybe you are inspired to ask your boss what you need to do to move up in the company.. Maybe you are inspired to have children or get married. Maybe you want to start feeding the homeless or loving on animals at an animal shelter. When you feel inspired, it is time to jump. Take those chances in life!

Don't forget to share your inspiration with others. Tell them what you are doing. Let the amazing support system you now have do its job by encouraging you and holding you accountable. If you see a terrific opportunity for one of your friends or colleagues tell them about it.

It is time to build each other up and stop tearing each other down. There is more than enough success to go around. We must let go of the belief we will only feel better if we are superior to others–with more money, a better car, a higher ranking at work. Happiness is not the same thing as superiority. Ever heard the adage, "It is lonely at the top?" Think about what it took to get to the top. How many people did you need to step on or crush under your overambitious feet? Of course, it's lonely at the top! Especially if you have to sever meaningful relationship to get there.

If this expression is not for you maybe you have heard the one about putting someone up on a pedestal. My theory has always been this: That pedestal better be big enough for all of us because if I am the only one up there, I am pulling everyone else up there with me. There is enough success for everyone. Everyone has unique goals and aspirations. Chase what inspires you. Resist the urge to hurt anyone along the way. Take them with you if they want to go, or respect what inspires them and makes them happy. It isn't hard to practice kindness. You will be happier on this path, rather than the path marked by the destruction of everyone around you.

Inspiration is an amazing thing. I was inspired twice in my life to become a college professor. I knew by the second time the light was lit, I had to follow the path. Now I am here. I truly love my job and my life.

I was recently headhunted to run a non-profit for almost twice the salary I make as a teacher. The funny thing is I never seriously considered it. I would never be as happy at work as I am now. Happiness far outweighs money. Some of you are reading this and cringing. It is okay if you are. Had I been inspired to chase this opportunity I would have. It is more than okay if you would have made the jump.

Part of the beauty of this world is we are all such unique people. Humanity is a truly beautiful tapestry of every imaginable color, faith, and culture. While one professional opportunity does not appeal to me, I know it will appeal to someone else and be a perfect, happy fit. We all are uniquely inspired. The important part is to recognize it and not hurt people in the process of finding it. Rather appreciate the people in your life and the role they are designed to play. I was born to be an educator and will always choose kindness with my students, colleagues and supervisors. Every single time.

What if you don't know what inspires you? What if you have never been inspired to throw kindness at someone or even professionally found your path? Ask! Ask your friends and family. Ask your teachers and coworkers. What do they see you doing in the future? What are your strengths and weaknesses? Remember these people love you! They will be honest even when you may or may not be ready to handle their honesty.

I have always been jealous of the marketable skills my friends and family have. They are always good at something. One of my best friends is an incredible artist, another is the best cook ever (I blame her solely for my fluff), and another is an amazing marketer (thank goodness I have her to help me with my horrible PR skills!). Another is an inspirational mother - I wish I had the patience to be. I say all I have is being ridiculously bubbly, and it is not marketable. Turns out I was wrong.

I am so fortunate to have people in my life who believe in me and encourage me. I cannot begin to stress the importance of having this in your life. You simply must find your people. You need them! My incredible support system told me how to embrace my bubbly spirit and make it my life mission. My friends, family, especially my mom, never ridiculed me. They lovingly supported me for who I already was.

Let me backtrack a little. Since I reached the age of truly embracing who I am - a little bit weird and definitely freakish, happy-people from all walks of life have asked me the same question, with different variations; how do I stay so positive all the time? It turns out there is a whole branch of psychology associated with this called Positive Psychology. I had found my niche.

From this point it feels like a whirlwind, I was invited to other parts of the country to give my aptly named "happy talk." Colleagues who I adore began to suggest I teach a class on Positive Psychology, and before I could even take a breath my first self-help book was in the works. The one you are reading right now.

I knew I wanted to be a professor, but I had no idea I would travel this path until my friends and family began to lead me. I am very inspired to see where this path leads and even more excited to see what's next. Find your inspiration. Seek advice from your loved ones and embark on your own unique path. I can't promise you will be rich with a house in the Hamptons, but you will be happy. You will be even happier if you sprinkle the path with your own unique brand of kindness confetti!

7. The Big, Ugly Carnivorous Monster

If you believe in yourself and have dedication and pride - and never quit, you'll be a winner. The price of victory is high but so are the rewards. Paul Bryant

People are bad. I understand you thought you purchased a feel good about everyone book, but the truth is the truth–people are bad. Christians call it a sin nature. We are forced to fight against evil for all eternity because of what happened in the Garden with Adam and Eve those many moons ago. Scholars have studied the phenomenon of evil for years. Regardless of what you call it, people are bad.

Famous psychological experiments have proven this time and time again. In 1961, Stanley Milgram, a prominent psychologist from Yale University, became obsessed with the events of World War II. More specifically, he wanted to know how Adolph Hitler was able to convince so many Germans turned Nazis into committing mass genocide against the Jewish people and other undesirables. After all, these are normal people like you and me, and you and I would surely never murder millions of people because of their religion... Or would we?

Milgram wondered if it was simple obedience to authority which allowed these atrocities to happen. He assembled a group of men no different from the everyday German during World War II, only this time here in America. Milgram found his study participants by listing a help wanted ad in the newspaper; recruiting male individuals for a psychological study to be conducted at Yale University. They were told the study was to find out how people learned. Obviously the participants were misled (we have new ethics rules in place now because of this). The participants ranged in ages 20-40, and professionally ranged from unskilled day laborers to successful professionals. They were given $4.50 just for showing up on the day of the experiment. This was very easy money for the time.

A participant was paired with a confederate participant on Milgram's payroll who knew what the experiment was truly about. The two men were placed in a room and told to draw straws to determine if they would be the "learner" or the "teacher." Unbeknownst to the newspaper recruited participants, this "random assignment" was staged, and the confederate was always the learner -the unaware newspaper participant always the teacher.

The learner, again, a paid employee of Stanley Milgram, introduced himself as "Mr. Wallace" and was led into a room where he was hooked up to an electric shock machine complete with electrodes to his arms. The uninformed participant was then led into another room containing a shock generator with a row of switches ranging from 15 volts (labeled as a "Slight Shock"), to 375 volts (labeled as "Danger: Severe Shock"), all the way up to 450 volts (labeled simply "XXX").

After "Mr. Wallace," was given an opportunity to memorize a list of word pairs, the "teacher" tested him by naming a word and asking the learner to recall its partner word from a list of four possible choices. The "teacher" was instructed by another confederate (On Dr. Milgram's payroll) wearing a white lab coat to administer an electric shock every time the learner made a mistake, increasing the level of shock with each incorrect answer.

"Mr. Wallace" gave mainly wrong answers (on purpose, of course), and for each of these incorrect choices, the" teacher" gave him an electric shock. When the "teacher" refused to administer a shock, the authority figure in the white lab coat gave him a series of predetermined prods to ensure the "teacher" continued.

There were four prods and if one was not obeyed, then the man in the white lab coat read out the next prod, and so on.

Prod 1: Please continue.
Prod 2: The experiment requires you to continue.
Prod 3: It is absolutely essential that you continue.
Prod 4: You have no other choice but to continue.

During this time, the "teacher" could hear "Mr. Wallace" becoming increasingly agitated. Starting with a simple ouch, his agitation grew to strong levels of discomfort, complaints of chest pain, and ultimately dead silence and a complete stop to answering the questions at all. At this point the man in the white lab coat reminded the "teacher" that no response is considered an incorrect response and the shock must be administered to continue.

I know what you are thinking. You would never go along with this simply because a man in a white lab coat was prodding you to continue however, the majority of the participants did go along with it. In fact, Stanley Milgram conducted this same study over and over again and the results remained consistent. 65 % (two-thirds) of the study participants went all the way to 450 volts simply because a presumed authority figure told them to, despite the fact the learner was in pain and possibly dead. 100% (every single participant), administered up to 300 volts, thus inflicting severe pain on a complete stranger, once again, just because a man in a coat told them too.

Stanley Milgram (1933-1984)

Of course, most of us would like to believe we do not have evil in our hearts. Although, if you are really honest with yourself, you will admit your brain has gone to some pretty dark places. Maybe you have fantasized about what you would like to do to your ex-boyfriend or ex-girlfriend after they broke your heart; or perhaps you have gotten creative with the torture of your particularly mean boss. Regardless, you know you are capable of evil thoughts.

The truth is everyone is capable of evil thoughts, and it is okay to own it. Everyone thinks about it, but rarely, does anyone act on it. Just like everything else, it would be hard to acknowledge, or even capitalize, on the good in your heart without first acknowledging the bad. So now that you have reminded yourself about the time you wanted to claw somebody's eyes out, think about how you didn't and how you overcame your bad human nature to become a positive, good human being. That is the person you can be proud of - the overcomer.

The more you embrace who you really are, the more pride you will have and the happier you will be when you choose the good path. The adage is true, you will never be truly happy until you love the true you - the you only those few chosen friends and family also know and love. Without self-pride, happiness will always be elusive. You have to actually like the person you are!

What if you don't like the person you are? Self-loathing is a rampant phenomenon in our society today. We use social media as a platform for comparison, and we wind up in a black pit of despair because we have just lost precious hours of our lives comparing ourselves to other people's highly filtered highlight reels. And it's not just social media. Self-loathing is still a battle for me, and I find myself comparing myself to others (in a very negative way), every chance I get–at school, at church, at conferences, at the store, you name it. Even in my car, I compare my home to other people's homes and my car to other people's cars. Here is what I have learned. Comparison and self-loathing are traps! You have got to find a way to shut those thoughts off. There are several tools helping you to love you as you should.

Keep Your Promises

If you love yourself, you respect yourself. One of the best ways to show respect to others is by keeping your promises to them. It is no different for yourself. If you promised yourself you were going to finish college, and you get your college degree, your pride increases. If you give up and let those perpetual stumbling blocks hinder your progress, your self-loathing will only continue to grow like a big, ugly carnivorous monster. You also must keep your promises to other people, the little ones and the big ones.

Keep your promises to your friends, your children, and your family. Modern society does little to respect promises. Take marriage for example. On our wedding day, we make promises to love, honor and cherish our spouses, but modern society does not foster these promises. Online pornography and random hookup websites hinder these promises from day one. Facebook helps us reconnect with lost friends and loved ones - there is no stronger curiosity than wondering about the path not taken.

I know people who lost their marriage because they had reconnected with a lost love. They became consumed with wondering what would had happened if they had married their high school or college sweetheart instead of their current spouse. I can tell you with 100% certainty I have never ever seen this situation end in a happily ever after situation. People change and grow. Your high school sweetheart is no longer the person you loved as a child. In fact, chances are you won't love them at all.

Keep the smaller promises too. If you promised to feed your friend's pets while they are on vacation, don't be a bad friend, actually do it. Nurture your relationships, don't destroy them just because you don't feel like doing something you promised to do. Keep your promises to your kids. If you promised your child a hoverboard if they pulled up their C's to A's, get your checkbook ready. If you cannot afford it, then don't make the promise to begin with.

Create and Complete a Daily List

Each day create a list of five things you are going to accomplish that day. Check them off one-by-one and complete the list every single day. This not only increases your pride, but your self-confidence and productivity as well.

Sometimes we need a lazy day, a day where we stay in our PJ pants and don't want to accomplish anything. Still make a list of five things and complete them. Even if they feel silly, like eat lunch, feed cats, take nap, watch Netflix, and eat dinner. You are still being productive and accomplishing something.

The problem with humanity is once we get off track we tend to stay off track. Take dieting for example. I am terrible about deciding to have a cheat day, for whatever reason -a holiday or on a trip. Regardless of the reason, once the decisions been made to cheat, it is nearly impossible for me to get back on the diet train. After all, I already cheated one day, I might as well enjoy the rest of the week and get back on my A-Game come Monday. Sound familiar? The problem is the longer we are off track the harder it is to get back on track. It is so much easier to go back for more cake.

Avoid Blaming Others and Making Excuses

Sometimes it is legitimately someone else's fault something did not get accomplished. A coworker or a teammate for a group presentation drops the ball and even though you did your part the project fails - although there was something you could have done to pick up the slack or cover for another. Believe me I know this is the worst. I cannot begin to tell you how many group presentations I have done on my own in my college experience because my teammates chose to be slackers. Remember this, you never know what someone else is going through.

Rather than blaming a colleague for dropping the ball on a major project, ask what you can do to help instead. This not only increases your pride, but it also strengthens your work relationships. You will be surprised to learn how often people aren't slacking, but going through personal battles or do not understand the assignment. Sometimes they are too embarrassed to ask for help. If you give it thought, you have probably been there too.

When my father passed away from cancer, I was only 18 years old. I dropped the ball on everything. Most people were wonderful. They held my hand and asked what they could do to make my life a little easier. However, I had one classmate who I overheard saying,

"Oh my God, she is going to use her dad dying to get away with everything…"

Do not be that person. Even if you have no idea what is going on, rather than getting angry or resentful, choose kindness. Reach out and see what you can do to make something easier on someone else. It will make your relationship better, and you will love how it makes you feel.

Stop Complaining

It is positively amazing, but did you know, historically speaking, no world problem has ever been solved by complaining? Completely astounding to learn something everyone does so much, has absolutely no positive effect whatsoever. Knowing this, why do we continue to do it?

Many people refer to complaining as venting. They need to get it out or surely death will occur. Once again, historically speaking, there have been no confirmed deaths by keeping your thoughts to yourself. It will not kill you, contrary to popular belief to just keep those thoughts in your head and let them go.

My mother used to say if you don't have anything nice to say, don't say anything at all. when did we decide to stop living by this principle and decide venting is a healthy thing? If you truly need to "get it out," you could always buy a journal or write it down and throw it away. Instead our entire society has embraced the concept that complaining is okay, even good. But let's take it a step further and really analyze what happens when you vent.

First of all, negativity breeds more negativity and hate breeds more hate. No human being has ever complained about someone and then liked them after the words were spoken. In fact, quite the opposite occurs. You spew negativity and then the friend you are venting your frustrations to validates your negativity, therefore deepening it, and the entire process makes everyone involved feel worse–angrier and more upset than they were to begin with.

If this wasn't bad enough, I am here to tell you some horrible truths. Human beings are terrible secret keepers. If you truly do not want a secret to be repeated, I recommend telling your dog, cat or even fish? Humans gossip, spill and sometimes gasp or exaggerate the story just because they want to make it juicier,

Have you ever played the childhood game Telephone? My extended family likes to play it at restaurants when we are waiting for our meals. We have far too many children between us and it is an incredible way to have all the children engaged and quiet. In this game, one person starts with a phrase or sentence, they whisper it to the person next to them, and the phrase or sentence goes down the line, or in our case, around the table. The last person to receive the phrase or sentence then shares the sentence out loud and everyone laughs because it has gotten so messed up. It is usually completely different from what the phrase or sentence originator said to begin with.

Complaining is a lot like the game of Telephone. You may originally have just shared your frustrations about a friend who hadn't been responding to your texts, but by the time it gets to the friend you have called her every number under the sun, and the friendship is ruined.

Life does not have to be this way. You can just stop complaining. Interesting fact, I have proposed this in class and in speaking engagements, and you might be horrified (or you might relate to) at the number of people who respond with,

"But what else is there to talk about?"

If this is you, may I suggest you find some new hobbies or find something striking your interest (please review "A World without Peanut Butter Cups"). I am definitely not saying you are a bad person, but I do think you could benefit from more joy in your life,

If you really need to get it out, write it down and throw it away, or at least put it in a journal you are 100% sure no one will ever read. If it is something particularly aggravating, you might want to consider writing it down and burning it, just please do not catch your house on fire. I would feel terrible.

I am not asking you to not express your feelings. Sometimes you are sad or angry or worried, and you absolutely should experience those fully. I am instead talking about the fruitless complaining. The type of complaining which turns into gossip and eventually destroys relationships.

If you truly cannot help but complain, may I recommend a therapist? There are great online therapists for one-time situations like these. You really do need to vent. The beautiful thing with therapists is they legally cannot repeat anything you have told them (unless you become a harm to yourself or others, or if they are forced to testify against you in a court of law). Furthermore, a therapist is trained to help you process what is happening in healthy ways. So, rather than venting and then continuing to stew in your own anger or frustration, you will process everything and be ready to move on from the situation.

Complaining truly accomplishes nothing positive. When overheard it harms relationships, and it hurts you as well. I once heard someone refer to complaining as taking poison and expecting the person you are complaining about to die. Things will happen to cause frustration or anger. It is how we respond to those situations that truly grows our character.

Challenge Yourself and Take Initiative

Is there something you have always wanted to do? Maybe go to graduate school, start a business, write a novel or become a foster parent? Challenge yourself to do it and initiate the process. Promise yourself you are going to do it, and you have created a golden ticket for pride.

I cannot begin to tell you the number of people who tell me they want to do something, but they just never start. My former pastor used to tell a story about a man who prayed every day to win the lottery. This went on for years and years and of course, the poor man never won the lottery. One day as the man was praying, once again to win the lottery, God finally had enough and came to pay him a visit,

"I can't make you win the lottery, if you never buy a ticket...."

It is up to us to buy the ticket, apply to graduate school, start writing or file the IRS paperwork to start a business. Don't be the person who just talks about doing something, and then lies on their deathbed years later regretting never taking the chance. Success will never come if you never leave your house, never meet those people and ultimately never try.

Even if you lose or fail, you will learn so much and be stronger because of it. Not to mention, you will also be armed with the knowledge of what not to do to get what you want. All of us fail but getting back on the horse is the most important next step. Take pride in your failure and take even greater pride in trying again.

It is also important to remember pride can be a good thing or a bad thing. Good pride represents our dignity and self-respect, while bad pride illustrates conceit and arrogance, and is usually experienced right behind a catastrophic failure. The type of pride necessary for happiness is called Authentic Pride. Without it happiness will be much harder to find.

Take into consideration, Marathoner Dean Karnazes who once ran 350 miles in just one marathon, and in another instance ran 50 marathons in 50 days. There is no doubt this man has some serious motivation; but where did it first come from?

On Dean's 30th birthday, he spent the day in reflection. He was reflecting on his life and his career- a promising position in sales. Despite professional success, he realized he didn't have anything he was actually very proud of. Dean began to run, but not just for the sake of running. It was something he had always wanted to do. He was ready for something, anything, in his life he could take pride in. Running became the source.

If you recently experienced a disappointment – maybe you were overlooked for a promotion at work, or your book was rejected by yet another publisher – and are feeling a distinct lack of pride, remember this is your fuel, your fuel for change! Use it to motivate yourself to make the changes you need to turn things around. Find something you've always wanted to do, something to take pride in. And do it.

Alternatively, if what you are currently doing does not give you a warm glow of authentic pride, perhaps it's time to reconsider your work life and strategies to happiness. In fact, even the happiest of us, myself included, could benefit from tuning into these feelings. If you don't feel good about what you are doing, happiness will remain elusive. I fully understand not everyone is in a position to change careers or move to another country, but everyone does have the ability to start SOMETHING - making them feel good about themselves.

One word of warning – if you've had a string of disappointments as of late and you're experiencing low feelings of pride exacerbated by feelings of low self-confidence and low self-esteem, you risk your absence of pride slipping into shame. Shame is a feeling of worthlessness. It can lead to depression or anxiety. Remember to always consult with a professional when it is needed.

8. I Don't Look Good In Prison Clothes

You become what you digest into your spirit. Whatever you think about, focus on, read about, talk about, you're going to attract more of into your life. Make sure they're all positive.
Germany Kent

Have you ever awakened in the morning and just knew it was going to be a bad day? Some people call it "waking up on the wrong side of the bed." Regardless of what you call it, you just have a gut feeling today is not going to be the best day ever. Not surprisingly the bad stuff all starts to happen- you stub your toe on the footboard of your bed. If you are like me, this episode alone results in a slew of explicatives and a subsequent undeniable bad mood. You go to work and your colleagues are in a bad mood; negative things seem to keep happening. You dribble coffee down your favorite shirt, you run your pantyhose, you accidentally click "reply all" on the worst possible email. You go home, and the dog has had several accidents on the carpet, your child has a F in Geometry, and your husband is looking at a potential lay off. If you have ever experienced anything like this, then you have survived a self-fulfilling prophecy. A self-fulfilling prophecy is when a person unknowingly and unwittingly causes a prediction to come true, due to the simple fact he or she expects it to come true.

In other words, expectations affect our behavior, which causes the expectation to be realized. For example, a high school softball coach expects freshmen players to be less skilled at the game, simply because they are younger. She does not put them in to play very often, and instead relies on her senior and junior players. When she does put them in, usually because the regular players have sustained injuries, they are rusty and don't do well, thereby fulfilling her expectations.

Perhaps this is where the adage came from: Expectation is nothing more than premeditated disappointment.

In one famous study of self-fulfilling prophecies, psychologists convinced a sample of male college students to believe a certain female student was attracted to them. A different sample of male students were told the same female student was not attracted to them. These social psychologists went on to observe interactions between the young men and the female in question. The research team concluded the woman was much more likely to act as if she was attracted to the first set of men, rather than the second. Why? Because the men who believed she was already attracted to them acted in a way which led her to actually be attracted to them.

Mind blowing isn't it? Our thoughts have more power than most people can possibly conceptualize. So, what are we really doing to ourselves when we stand in front of the bathroom mirror obsessing over our flaws, or telling ourselves we will never be out of debt? We are manifesting these things into reality! Some psychologists call this mental or creative imagery, and many studies and books have been written on this subject. However, we still keep doing this to ourselves-ultimately creating our own misery.

So, what if we stopped? What if we became self-aware and actively engaged with our thoughts? What if every time we looked in the mirror thinking, "Ugh I still look pregnant and my baby is 12 years old" we instead stop ourselves and say something like, "Wow, I look amazing for a working mom!" or just "I look amazing!" Here's the truth. When you do this people will look at you and think you look amazing, because you are amazing.

Think about how much your life could change armed with this knowledge! One of my favorite things to do every morning is to choose a daily mantra. One mantra I use frequently is:

Today is going to be the happiest day of my life! Maybe it is an ordinary day, but when you feel good about the ordinary it becomes extraordinary. What was before a normal business lunch becomes the best sushi you have ever had coupled with so much laughter you leave the meeting still smiling.

I recently asked my students to come up with their favorite happiness mantras, maybe some of these will resonate with you:

- "Whatever does not kill me makes me stronger." - Nietzsche
- People are just as happy as they make up their minds to be... So today I choose to be happy!
- Knowing that if Plan A fails, there is still 25 other letters to try.
- I don't look good in prison clothes. I don't look good in prison clothes.... (I cannot lie, this one was my favorite of the bunch, I mean really, who looks good in horizontal stripes?)
- Do something that makes you happy!!!!!!!!
- Life is short, don't waste it.
- Live! Live! Live!

Every single one of these, puts a smile on my face, and brightens my day.

Like many of the things you have read about in this book, this one has not always been easy for me. In fact, I even described myself as the personal embodiment of Murphy's Law and then there's my Travel Curse. I know on some level I am attracting the travel curse on myself by believing it is going to happen well before it actually does.

Just think what we could accomplish if we utilized the phenomenon to completely reshape our own existences far beyond setting the tone for the day, feeling better about ourselves. If my brain is powerful enough to conjure up a travel curse, what else could it possibly attract my way?

Hundreds of years ago the Law of Attraction was first thought to have been shared to humanity by Buddha. Many scholars believed he wanted it to be known, "What you have become is what you have thought."

This belief is the very core of the Law of Attraction. This concept spread throughout Western culture and came to be known as Karma, a belief popular in many societies, both religious and nonreligious.

In the centuries to follow it would become a common understanding among many:

"You reap what you sow."

In other words, whatever you put out in this world (whether it is anger or happiness, hate or love) is ultimately what you receive in your own life. This simple and easy-to-follow concept has been popular among many for a number of years. It demonstrates the idea of the power of attraction, or mindfulness as it is frequently called today. This concept is not new age, or even new, it is something embraced by the majority of humankind, and continues to have a stronghold on our very concept of morality.

The main principles of the Law of Attraction can also be discovered in the teachings of many civilizations and religions. For example, in Proverbs 23:7, it reads:

"As a man thinks in his heart, so is he."

Proof that the Law of Attraction works has been published and shared over and over, all just waiting for humankind, regardless of religion, to discover and enjoy.

The Law Of Attraction and its values have been seen throughout history. Many successful and respected men and women who have left a tremendous impact on the world give or gave credit to this process for their success in life. Many well-known poets, artists, scientists and great thinkers such as Shakespeare, Blake, Emerson, Newton and Beethoven all conveyed this message through their many works, stressing the significance of how being mindful can ultimately change your life.

Advocates for the Law of Attraction continue to rise in status in success. Some of the more modern success stories include Oprah Winfrey, Jim Carrey, and Denzel Washington. In addition, with over 7 million Facebook followers, there are plenty of success stories surrounding the Law Of Attraction you can spend countless hours enjoying.

Choosing happiness is much easier when we understand the universe is on our side. The more time you spend becoming aware of your thoughts, and keeping them positive, the more fulfilling and rewarding your life can be.

Using this incredible tool can promote positive change in almost every area of your life. Oftentimes, we think we know what our life is missing in order to be happy. If you are convinced you have this figured out, go ahead and give it a try!

Mindfulness and Love

There is only one happiness in this life, to love and be loved.
George Sand

Sometimes it feels like everyone except you has life figured out. They all have perfect lives, perfect jobs, perfect homes, and perhaps most importantly the perfect love. It is positively exhausting to date person after person trying to find "the one." Trust me I know I have been there. I actually have never liked dating and have always preferred serious relationships, but with this theory you wind up investing in what may or may not be a lasting relationship. This is perhaps even more emotionally exhausting than dating.

Trust me when I say it is completely normal to want to give up. I cannot begin to tell you how many times I have told my mom I was throwing in the towel and committing myself to the crazy cat lady life. Maybe you too have resigned yourself to the single life, even though you know deep down you still yearn for love and companionship. The good news is the Law of Attraction can help!

If you're going to manifest your soulmate with your thoughts, it is absolutely crucial to understand what you have been doing wrong so far. You may be ultimately blocking yourself from creating the romance you have always dreamed of. Think carefully and determine if any of the following are true for you:

- You have unconsciously shut down. After too many hurts and disappointments, it is common to build a wall around your heart to protect it from future pain.
- You have unfinished business. It is impossible to find a new love, if you have not gotten over your last love.
- You have lost faith. Many people stop believing an actual soulmate exists, and they choose to settle instead for being alone. As I have said before - do not settle!

If any of these are you, it is important to address it before you can move on with the process.

When you are ready, the first step is to let the universe know exactly what you are looking for. This is done by designing your dream partner. Be very careful not to think about what you don't want, because then you are putting those thoughts out too. Remain only focused on what you are looking for. Keep in mind there is no such thing as a perfect person,. Be willing to develop love with someone who is perfect for you, despite his or her flaws. Remember you have flaws too!

Next, you must learn to love yourself. The old adage is true; you are so much easier to love when you already love yourself. Make time for self-care and treat yourself the way you want your partner to treat you in the future.

Most importantly, don't give up and don't forget to trust the process.

Mindfulness and Wealth

The greatness of a man is not in how much wealth he acquires, but in his integrity and his ability to affect those around him positively. Bob Marley

For no reason whatsoever do I believe happiness is equated with wealth. However, I do realize without being able to eat or put a roof over your head, happiness will always remain a distant fantasy.

One of the easiest ways to attract money is to focus on what you do have rather than what you don't. If you keep telling yourself you are drowning in bills or will never get out of debt, you are attracting more of the same - bills and debt. Instead it is crucial to focus on the abundance, what your life would look like if you were not overwhelmed by financial anxiety.

Perhaps you have always wanted to build your credit so you can move from the rental home in which your family is squashed, into a home of your own with enough room to be comfortable. Rather than complaining about how small your current residence is, start focusing on what it would be like to have the home you are dreaming about. What colors would you paint? What furniture would you buy? Focus on what you want, not what you don't want.

This is also a great place to use those mantras we love! Some of my favorite mantras include:

- Making money is easy!
- I love living debt free!
- I have a successful, wonderful life!

Even if the mantra isn't true today, you are putting these positive thoughts into the universe to attract these very things to you!

Mindfulness and Health

I believe that the greatest gift you can give your family and the world is a healthy you. Joyce Meyer

With insanely busy work lives, commitments to friends and family and general everyday life stressors, we often neglect our own personal health. While using The Law of Attraction cannot replace a healthy diet, exercise and regular doctor visits, it can promote a wide array of benefits for your mental, spiritual and physical health. It has been acknowledged within modern medicine the 'placebo effect' is a very real phenomenon. This idea demonstrates the magnitude of importance the mind has in the physical recovery of the body. It has illustrated to the entire world the astonishing capabilities of the mind in its ability to convince itself and the body into a state of total health, without any external intervention.

However, it is vital to know I am in no way advocating for you to stop your routine doctor visits or throw away your prescriptions. I am talking about combining traditional medicine with mindfulness to create the best positive version of you.

Whether we are aware of it or not, our brain is continuously in play with the conditions of our physical body. In fact, oftentimes our body does things just to let our brain know something is wrong and requires attention. In regard to mindfulness and your health, it is imperative to remove any barriers to this communication to live an optimal life.

- Eliminate stress whenever possible. Research suggests emotional turmoil when built up over time will spill over causing physical turmoil. One of my favorite tricks when I start to feel stressed out is to ask myself, "Will this matter next month?" You will be shocked to discover how often the answer is no,

- Improve your self-image and start using positive thinking. Again, this is a matter of thinking about what you want, rather than what you don't. If you are telling yourself you will always be fat. Guess what? You will always be fat. If you start loving the way you look now, it will increase to positive developments in your health.

- Remember a healthy mind creates a healthy body. If you are sad, stressed, anxious or worried, these will all cause a negative impact on your physical health. Choosing happiness allows you to not only feel better emotionally. but physically as well.

I am a firm believer in the Law of Attraction; what we think will happen, will happen. I am not generally materialistic; I don't really care if my car is brand new, my purse has a label or I live in the biggest house on the block, however I do love success and positivity. I am happiest when I am doing the things I love.

Not too terribly long ago, I decided to put this to the test. I wanted to become a fulltime tenure track professor. I knew the money wasn't great, but I was always happiest in my classrooms as an adjunct - it never felt like I was even working. I remembered learning about something called creative visualization, and I decided to try it out. Every day I set aside five minutes to imagine my life as a full-time professor. I pictured my office and how it was decorated. I pictured my students engaging with me and having four years with them rather than one semester. I imagined conversations with colleagues. I even imagined what I would wear (not too different from what I wore before I became a college professor).

And then something remarkable happened. I was offered three different tenure-track positions at three different universities, one of which I accepted! Did I truly "think this into existence"? I guess I will never know for sure, but it has definitely become a practice to regularly imagine my life the way I want it. It surely has not hurt!

I have begun to extend this practice in every imaginable way. When I go to the store, I start singing about "Chrissy's Princess Parking" before I even get there, and you know what, you are reading a book written by the girl who has gotten the first space at Wal-Mart on Black Friday several years running!

I have also begun the practice of doodling in a sketchbook of things I want to happen. I am so not a talented artist (Bestie Rachel has that honor), but it is super fun to go back and cross off the things I doodled after they have actually happened..

I know very few people who are really happy with the way their life looks. Most people are always thinking the key to happiness is more. More success, more accomplishments, more stuff. What they don't realize is by focusing their energies in this way, they are missing out on all the happiness right in front of them!

One of the most dangerous things you can do is keep your happiness in the future. For example:

- I will be happy when... This one is extremely dangerous for several reasons. First and foremost, it keeps your happiness locked in the future and not in the present. It is also placing an irrational amount of power on one thing. It may or may not happen. Even if it does happen, you have no idea what it really looks like. You can be super excited about finding a new job, but whether the job will be the right fit will never be determined until you are in the job for the amount of time necessary to be comfortable. Please take your happiness out of the future.

- I will be happy if…. Again, unless you are clairvoyant, placing all of your happiness hopes into an "if statement" is incredibly risky. I often hear people saying I will be happy if I meet my soulmate. I hate to be the bearer of bad news, but I can tell you I have met more people who have thought they had met their soulmate. It made them unhappier than ever.

It is crucial to embrace the here and now and grasp the happiness embedded in the tiny moments. If you remain fixed on the future as your only source of happiness, it will remain there - in the future, and never in your present.

Maybe you are waiting on a dream job. Between the resume tweaking and job searching, what are you doing? Are you feeling depressed it is taking so long or losing your self-worth? If you are, what are you missing? Precious moments with your friends and family? Time to visit and spend time with the people who always seem to be placed on the back burner? Embrace that beautiful filler time! The dream job will come (with persistence and hard work), but those moments in the middle are the ones which bring pure joy.

9. Maintaining Happiness

Today I choose life. Every morning when I wake up I can choose joy, happiness, negativity, pain... To feel the freedom that comes from being able to continue to make mistakes and choices - today I choose to feel life, not to deny my humanity but embrace it. Kevyn Aucoin

Now that you have found happiness, it is important to not let it go. Learning to love yourself and be happy with yourself, opens the door to so many incredible things–successful marriages, vocational joy, and cherishing virtually every moment.

Over the years, I have worked with people diagnosed with serious mental illnesses; such as depression, anxiety, bipolar disorder, schizophrenia and schizoaffective disorder. While it is not important you understand what each of these illnesses looks like, it is important you see the common thread. Each of these illnesses are treatable with medication - medications continues to get better and improve over time. The problem with mental illness and procuring happiness is you begin to feel good, and immediately think, "This is incredible! I am cured!"

As much as this is a dangerous assumption for an individual with a mental illness, it is also a dangerous assumption for someone who has recently chosen happiness. For both, maintenance is key. You have found what works for you, now you must keep doing it. Nothing happens in a vacuum. You cannot call yourself an amazing mother because you spent one hour doing homework with your child one time, and then spent the rest of his or her life ignoring her. Happiness, like everything great, takes hard work and commitment.

There's an App For That!

Like everything else in today's society there is an app for maintaining happiness. My personal favorite is Happify. The best part - it's free. Happify uses evidence-based practices (hooray for science!) to create games and activities proven to reduce stress, build self-confidence and eliminate negativity. It has great reviews, and many users report feeling happier in just a few days after installing the app on their smartphones.

Force A Smile

Even if you're unhappy, just pretend that you're happy. Eventually, your smile will be contagious to yourself. I had to learn that. Evangeline Lilly

Let's play a little game. What I want you to do is smile. Right now. Don't just smile, smile a huge, ridiculous, over the top smile. Now hold it. While you are holding it, think about something which makes you either angry or sad. Be careful! Make sure your smile remains a smile and does not become a grimace.

Was it hard? I have had students, friends, colleagues, and conference attendees not only tell me it is hard, but many report it is impossible to feel angry or sad feelings when you are smiling. This is true for me. I find it impossible to remember a single sad or angry fact when I am smiling.

Call it 'fake it until you make it' or whatever you want, research suggests if you just keep smiling (even if it is completely forced), you will feel happier. Trust me. My coworkers and friends usually know when I am having a horrible day. I am sitting in my office with the worst forced smile possible, but it works. I eventually wind up laughing at myself and feeling better.

Daily Mantra

Most of us start out with a positive attitude and a plan to do our best. Marilu Henner

Like the ones my students gave me, I love to come up with a daily mantra, and use it throughout the day. You can write it in dry erase marker on your bathroom mirror or put little notes with your mantra written on it where you look throughout the day–your refrigerator, your computer, your phone, your wallet, etc. Some of my favorite daily mantras include:

- Today is the happiest day ever.
- Today I will take action towards the person I want to be.
- Today I will live beautifully and love completely.
- I have enough, I do enough and I am enough.
- I do not fear the fire, I am the fire.

Some call these positive affirmations, and research suggests they lead to better life satisfaction, and better outcomes in general. Much like the self-fulfilling prophecies, you are what you think you are. If you are writing on the mirror, I will never get the job I want, then you will never get the job you want. If you write on the mirror, I am owning this interview, chances are good you will do exactly that.

Vision Boards

The mind is the limit. As long as the mind can envision the fact that you can do something, you can do it, as long as you really believe 100 percent. Arnold Schwarzenegger

Along the same lines, research suggests putting your goals, or anything happy, directly in your line of sight, makes it more obtainable. Buy a corkboard, or at least some high-quality poster board and begin adding pictures to it.. These pictures can be anything you want, and yours will be unique. That is part of the beauty of the human existence. Some things on my vision board include:

- Photographs of my family and friends
- Photographs of my cats (yes, I am a crazy cat lady!)

- Pictures of Hello Kitty
- Mementos from cherished memories (ticket stubs from Six Flags or the boarding pass from an amazing trip.)
- Pictures of cats that aren't my cats (feel free to take note of the recurring theme)
- Pictures or flyers from the college I teach at or work events which were incredible.
- Pictures of things I would like to do with my home (furniture and remodeling)
- Places I want to go (someday I will get to Paris!)

These are only suggestions, make it your own, and most importantly display it prominently!

Transform a Negative into a Positive

Today I choose life. Every morning when I wake up I can choose joy, happiness, negativity, pain... To feel the freedom that comes from being able to continue to make mistakes and choices - today I choose to feel life, not to deny my humanity but embrace it. Kevyn Aucoin

As I have said before this is easier said than done. We are all quite comfortable in our misery and feeling good about ourselves is foreign to the point of socially unacceptable. In today's culture, if you are comfortable being a little bit fluffy and love yourself the way you are, you are fat shamed into believing you cannot be happy unless you are a size 4. It is borderline taboo to embrace the unique person you are and love yourself. You are EXPECTED to berate yourself and compare yourself to others.

Just stop. You do not have to be a size 4. You do not have to berate and compare yourself. It is not only perfectly fine to love yourself, but it's one of the single best gifts you can give yourself other than another cat (kidding, kinda).

Try to do this as much as you can. Eventually there will be no more negatives to turn into positives. In fact, don't stop with just yourself, try it with talking to other people too. When I was a little girl, my parents would tell me,

"If you don't have anything nice to say, then don't say anything at all."

Truer words were never spoken. I once had a friend tell me if she didn't vent about the coworker she hated she would "just explode." I had to break it to her gently that it has never been documented for someone to die in such a fashion. She did not appreciate my humor. That being said, it is true. No one has ever died from not saying something negative they were thinking. Conversely, if you think something nice, you should always say it. Why would you intentionally deprive someone of a blessing? Furthermore, you never really know what someone is going through. Why not be the light in their darkness?

Make a Gratitude List

"Gratitude unlocks the fullness of life. It turns what we have into enough." Melodie Beatty

Placing yourself into an attitude of gratitude will bring about, not only greater happiness, but more life satisfaction as well. When I suggest the gratitude journal to people, it is too daunting for some to begin, and even more difficult for some to maintain. So, if you are among those who feel completely overwhelmed, at least initially, by the gratitude journal, make it easier on yourself.

Place a notepad or notebook next to your bed. Before you go to sleep, write a list of three things which happened [that day] for which you are grateful. When you wake up in the morning, before you check your phone (in fact, I don't believe your phone should even be in your bedroom!), reread your 3 things from the previous day and set the tone for the new day. Repeat this. Somedays it will be easy and some days it will be very difficult. If you need ideas:

- Your Family
- Your Friends
- Your Bed
- Your Home
- Your Sense of Sight
- Your Sense of Hearing
- Your Job
- Your Money
- Your Pets
- Your Car

Again, the possibilities are endless. And you know far better than me the things in your life you are the most grateful for!

The Happiness Clicker

Perhaps you have heard of Ivan Pavlov and classical conditioning? Ivan Pavlov was a Russian physiologist best known in the discipline of psychology for his discovery of classical conditioning. During his studies on the digestive systems of dogs, Pavlov noted the animals naturally salivated upon the presentation of food. However, he soon realized the animals began to salivate whenever they saw the white lab coat of an experimental assistant. It was through this observation Pavlov discovered by associating the presentation of food with the lab assistant, a conditioned response occurred. This discovery had a huge influence on psychology, and Pavlov was also able to demonstrate that the animals could be conditioned to salivate to the sound of a bell.

If you think about it, we classically condition ourselves regularly. We create new associations in our brain not there before, but once created they tend to stick around. For example, have you ever had food poisoning from a restaurant? It was probably brutal, with violent vomiting and incessant wishing for an instantaneous death. A year later, a friend or colleague recommends going to the same restaurant. How do you react?

If you are like most people, you are probably nauseous at the very thought. In fact, most people never return to the restaurant that infected them. There is a new association between feeling viciously ill and the restaurant where it happened. If creating that association was easy and basically unintentional, what if we could apply the same principle to our own lives?

There was once a college student, I will call her Sarah. Sarah was the nicest, sweetest young lady in the program at her particular university. She was very well liked by her friends, peers, teachers, and classmates. She always managed to stay abundantly happy, but only the psychology majors truly knew what kept her smiling.

Sarah carried around a small dog clicker. Small enough to be tucked into a pocket and taken, quite literally, everywhere. Every time Sarah had a happy thought or was just feeling happy, she clicked her "happiness clicker." Eventually, Sarah had classically conditioned herself to feel happy at the sound of virtually any click. This enabled her to feel positive the majority of the time and lead a happy existence. All with the click of a button.

10. Long Term Happiness

Happiness radiates like the fragrance from a flower and draws
all good things towards you. Maharishi Mahesh Yogi

So, you have embraced the happiness mantras, vision boards,
and mindfulness, but maybe you are still resistant, asking
yourself can this really last forever? The answer is
ABSOLUTELY. Once you have embraced the basic tenets of
happiness, you can begin the process of procuring lifelong
happiness.

We, as human beings, have an awful tendency of putting
our happiness in the hands of other people–our spouse, our
children, our friends, our family, and even our coworkers. An
important thing to remember is happiness is a lifelong journey
beginning and ending with you!

So, if you thought you were done, lifelong happiness has
only just begun. The good part is once you have done all of this
work, the rest should be a piece of cake. In fact, I can
summarize lifelong happiness into three words–Love, Purpose,
and Selflessness.

Love

There is only one happiness in this life, to love and be loved.
George Sand

We have already discussed the importance of having a
strong support system and friends making you want to be a
better person, but what about love? I am not trying to tell you a
single person will never achieve true happiness, because it isn't
true.. However, I will tell you lasting happiness demands on
loving and being loved.

Have you ever felt like no one loved you? Or perhaps even wondered if you were unlovable? Feelings such as these leave deep gaping holes in our hearts and are far more painful than a break up or divorce. Love is more than intimacy and even marriage. The kind of love I am talking about stretches out to the reaches of parents, cousins, siblings, friends, and those around you who care for you. It's the people in the world who offer complete and utter support, regardless of how bold, fragile, or doomed-to-fail the thing you're working on is.

I never claim to be perfect, in fact, I often tell people I never mess up in small ways, I always mess up in huge, gigantic ways - ways in which most people's lives begin to crumble. There are so many instances in my life when I made decisions so shameful I do my best to hide them from the people I love; out of fear they will no longer love me.

The truth is it is in these moments we realize who truly loves us. Those who are willing to watch us mess up and still continue to love and support us through the whole mess and on the other side of the mess truly love us.

As I explain to students, our brains are hard-wired to only see the world from a single perspective, and this perspective is our own. Have you ever wondered why your loved ones do not actually listen when you give them advice? Perhaps you have a friend in a relationship with a woman who is a complete gold digger. You tell your friend over and over again this is the case and this woman is surely using him. However, he does not want to hear it. They are in love, he says, and of course, you are wrong about her true intentions.

Of course, you are not wrong, I find we rarely are, and eventually this friend is calling you telling you how right you were and lamenting having not listened to you. Sound familiar? At this point, you are at a crossroads. You can be angry at said friend for not listening to you, or you can understand this as part of the human existence and love him through his turmoil.

This is the kind of love which promotes lifelong happiness. The kind that watches you mess up and loves you anyway. This kind of love does not celebrate, "I told you so." rather it just is what it is, actual love, and, with love like this you can achieve anything.

Purpose

If you're alive, there's a purpose for your life. Rick Warren

"I'm sorry, son, but your vision is just not good enough for what we are looking for in the Navy" said the Recruitment Officer as he closed the door on the way out of the room.

These words, spoken to my husband, many years ago, crushed his soul and broke his heart. For as long as he could remember, he had dreamed of having a career in the Navy, and he never dreamed\ his poor vision would be the undoing of decades of planning his life around this career.

Sitting alone in a tiny office at the Naval Academy where he desperately wanted to be, he broke down in tears. He was seventeen. His life was still ahead of him, but in that moment, it was over. His hopes, dreams, and aspirations all shattered by one sentence, from a man who had no idea how much he wanted this.

In the following months, he fell in and out of depression. He was in a downward spiral descending into one of the deepest and darkest pits he would ever find myself in. There was nothing for him to get out of bed for. He wasn't walking the path towards his mountain.

His purpose was gone.

I would love to say this was nothing but a brief period in my husband's life, but, unfortunately it wasn't. He tried everything he could to fill the gaping void where his dreams once were, but nothing was fulfilling, until he found the field of rehabilitation.

Rehabilitation was all about helping people like him. People who had their dreams squashed by a physical or emotional limitation they had never expected. My husband had found a field where he could use his hardships to help others achieve their dreams or create new ones.

And suddenly, he was well again. He was happy, and he was back to being Matthew Madison once again.

I have seen this happen with him, and I have seen it happen with many others. Losing your purpose in life is depressing and potentially debilitating for so many. When someone has lost all direction and continues to walk on a road aimlessly to nowhere, they become despondent and any happiness they had been able to achieve begins to disappear.

Truly happy people, as in the lifelong happy people, (not the ones possessing fleeting happiness) have a clear path of where they are going. They have something for which they are living for, something to strive for, something to eventually attain and make their very own.

It doesn't have to be career-based. it can be a passion for anything–being a parent, recycling, absolutely anything you want. In order to focus on being happy, you must take the time to sit down and identify what it is you want to do. What you love to do. What gives you purpose.

You need to figure out what makes you feel like the best version of yourself!

Selflessness

If selfishness is the key to being miserable, then selflessness must be the key to being happy! Joyce Meyer

Selflessness is going above and beyond your own self, to facilitate happiness in another. If you are familiar with Maslow's Hierarchy of Needs, this is the part of happiness which is self-actualization.

Selflessness occurs when you have grown beyond your own needs, you feel safe and secure, you have love and belonging, and you have learned to love yourself. This is the part of life when you realize true happiness is only achieved in securing happiness for others.

Earlier, I had talked about throwing kindness like confetti. This is bigger, more meaningful and more existential in nature. You have found yourself, and now you want to give this gift to others, selflessly.

Many people believe there is no true altruism. I can agree on some level because everyone knows how amazing it feels to do something wonderful for someone who will never be able to thank you. This feeling itself is your reward, and, therefore, there is no real altruism. I am ok with this because the feeling is better than any drug or high (at least I imagine) and perhaps even more addictive.

Our lives can be lived for any number of reasons. They can be used to advance a personal agenda for selfish, or at least egocentric reasons. Some of the reasons include: money, possessions, fame, prestige, or simply a good reputation. However, our lives can also be lived for the pursuit of justice, happiness, or growth for other people.. We can live to solve the issues which we encounter in this world. We can dedicate ourselves to advancing ideals, the same ones which light the fire in us - that fuels our passion. Only when we embrace this mindset of service to others and selflessness will we find lasting happiness in our world.

Many try to define success in terms of winning over others, having power over others, or the ability to dominate others. Some define success in terms of stuff, having more money in the bank, the bigger house, the better vacation and the fancier car. The lust for power and accumulation is an epidemic in today's society. Rather than deriving joys by standing for others, we take the greatest pleasure in ordering others around, having the power to make decisions impacting others and the right to own what others cannot.

This type of happiness is short-lived. It will always fade. Nobody is intimately drawn to selfishness. Nobody seeks the wise counsel of a selfish person. Nobody is willing to give themselves up for one who desires his own wishes above all things.

However, we are inexplicably drawn to those who selflessly give of themselves. Those who love and give generously find a type of fulfillment which extends beyond position or title. They have an influence which reaches into our heart and soul. Their example is studied. Their counsel is sought. Their stories are told in positive ways. And their happiness is truly lasting.

Happiness is attainable for all people. It is not limited to the thin, the beautiful or the rich. You just have to want it and be willing to choose it in your life. I truly hope this journey begins for you today. I hope you choose happiness.

Today, as opposed to my teenage years, I am a happy, somewhat well-adjusted 40-year old mom, wife, friend, and colleague. I do not always have good days, in fact some are worse than others. But, what matters is I have learned to deal with unpleasant situations and see the good in the bad. Everyone does not like me, and that's ok too. I like me. I think I am pretty funny, cool and smart.

When I reflect back on my childhood, I am happy I never committed suicide and I stayed the course. I know every single experience led me to become the woman I am today.

Just a few weeks ago, I celebrated my 40th birthday. A 40th birthday is an interesting milestone because I believe we all tend to spend a good chunk of the day reflecting on what we have accomplished, and what we have yet to dream. I spent my day surrounded by family and friends. So many friends we had to break up the day into several events to accommodate those who wanted to celebrate with me.

I have come a long way from the little girl who cried and believed no one loved her. My wish for you is to be surrounded by all the love and happiness you can imagine.

Appendix A

If you would like some additional reading….

Beckwé, M., Deroost, N., Koster, E., De Lissnyder, E., & De Raedt, R. (2014). Worrying and rumination are both associated with reduced cognitive control. Psychological Research, 78(5), 651-660.

Cuddy, A. C., Wilmuth, C. A., Yap, A. J., & Carney, D. R. (2015). Preparatory Power Posing Affects Nonverbal Presence and Job Interview Performance. Journal of Applied Psychology, 100(4).

Fredrickson, B. L. (2009). Positivity. New York: Crown.

Froman, L. (2009). Positive Psychology in the Workplace. Journal of Adult Development.

Boukes M, Vliegenthart R. (2017). News consumption and its unpleasant side effect: Studying the effect of hard and soft news exposure on mental well-being over time. Journal of Media Psychology: Theories, Methods, And Applications.

Watson, E. (NDS). Tips to Stay positive in negative situations. And anything by Craig Groeschel!

About the Author

Dr. Chrissy Whiting-Madison was born and raised in Johnstown, Pennsylvania. She received her Bachelor of Arts in Psychology from Saint Vincent College in Latrobe, Pennsylvania, and, shortly afterward, relocated to Tulsa, Oklahoma. She obtained her Masters' degree in Rehabilitation Counseling from Langston University-Tulsa, and later her Doctorate (PhD) in Rehabilitation from the University of Arkansas.

Chrissy currently serves as Assistant Professor of Psychology at Rogers State University in Claremore, Oklahoma. She also continues to practice as a therapist and specializes in Positive Psychology.

Chrissy currently resides in Sperry, Oklahoma with her husband, Matt, her daughter, Carina, her three bonus children, Gabriel, Joshua and Emma, and their beloved 5 cats. Chrissy loves scary movies, Hello Kitty and spending time with all of her loved ones.

You can connect with Chrissy on Facebook:
Dr. Chrissy Whiting-Madison-Author

www.ingramcontent.com/pod-product-compliance
Lightning Source LLC
LaVergne TN
LVHW020047160726
843469LV00043B/1548